Best Shropshire Walks

Les Lumsdon

Copyright © L.M. Lumsdon, 1996

Reprinted 1998

Published by Sigma Leisure – an imprint of
Sigma Press, 1 South Oak Lane, Wilmslow, Cheshire SK9 6AR, England.

British Library Cataloguing in Publication Data
A CIP record for this book is available from the British Library.

ISBN: 1-85058-484-2

Typesetting and Design by: Sigma Press, Wilmslow, Cheshire.

Cover photograph: The Long Mynd *(Scenesetters, Little Stretton)*

Maps: Pam Upchurch

Printed by: MFP Design and Print

Disclaimer: the information in this book is given in good faith and is believed to be correct at the time of publication. No responsibility is accepted by either the author or publisher for errors or omissions, or for any loss or injury howsoever caused. Only you can judge your own fitness, competence and experience.

Contents

18: Market Drayton 89
Very easy walking along tracks, roads and canal tow-path.
Distance: 5 miles (8km)

19: Morville 93
A gentle walk along a valley of the Mor Brook.
Distance: 2 miles (3.5km). Add a further 1½ miles for the extension.

20: Much Wenlock 97
Through fields into Corvedale returning by way of Wenlock Edge.
Distance: 7 miles (11km)

21: The Munslows 101
Fine walking over Wenlock Edge between two quiet villages. Several steady climbs.
Distance: 4 miles (6.5km)

22: Myddle 105
Easy walking around Shropshire villages.
Distance: 5 miles (8km)

23: Neen Sollars and Cleobury Mortimer 109
A rewarding walk in undulating dairy country.
Distance: 7 miles (11km)

24: Newcastle 114
A harder walk that includes a section along the Offa's Dyke path.
Distance: 6 miles (9.5km)

25: Newport 118
A very gentle walk along well-used footpaths with features of interest en route.
Distance: 4½ miles (7km)

26: Oswestry Race Course 121
A mixture of scenery from gentle pasture and parkland to thickly wooded slopes.
Distance: 7 miles (11km)

27: Pontesbury 126
Paths and old farm tracks.
Distance: 8 miles (10-11km)

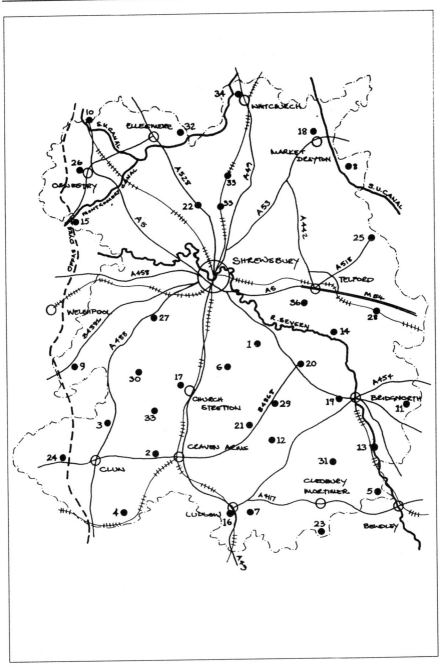

The Subtle Beauty of Shropshire

Of the border counties Shropshire holds the greatest promise for the walker. From wild, heather hills and wooded scarps to gentle riverside paths and green lanes once trodden by travelling folk, the subtle beauty of the Shropshire landscape begins to unfold.

The Epitome of England

Enticing though the Shropshire hills may be, the County offers far more. It is, after all, the largest inland county and stretches from a point south of Ludlow virtually to the Potteries and from the fringes of the West Midlands conurbation to the western slopes of Clun Forest. Within this area there is a variety of landscapes, a point so eloquently made by an editor of the well-respected Murray's Travel Companion in the late 1870s:

'Salop can be considered an epitome of England, for it contains within the compass of a few miles all the characteristics of an Alpine district in miniature, while at the same time within sight of orchards, gardens and farmhouses.'

Could we say different now?

The Great Divider

The Severn is a great divider. Roughly speaking the land area to the north is a gently undulating plain, but not without highlights. The underlying rock is mainly New Red sandstone and the ridges such as Harmer, Grinshill and Weston offer fine local viewpoints. Of course, The Wrekin is something special. Although not that high (1334 feet), it is a very distinctive landmark which people genuinely cherish. It is a break point between the plain and the Severn itself as it makes its way, hurriedly, through the Ironbridge gorge.

Meres

It is also a locality characterised by meres, particularly in North Shropshire. These natural lakes, brought about in post-glacial times when large flows of melting ice gouged out hollows and deposited in return clayey layers, are welcome retreats for wildlife and offer in many places lovely shorter strolls for the rambler. Hence the area is often referred to as 'The Little Lakeland of Shropshire'.

Easy walking in the Severn Valley!

West of Oswestry

To the west of Oswestry, however, the landscape becomes far more dramatic with high ground and plunging valleys, indistinguishable from Wales, marked only by occasional road signs and the centuries old Offa's Dyke. This is borderland and is rich in landscape and heritage. The Iron Age Camp at Oswestry really is a must to visit.

South of The Severn

South of the Severn, the landscape is more varied. Not only do you find the delightful valleys of the Corve, Rea, Onny and Teme but also more undulating farmland sweeping away from the Clee Hills, the Wyre Forest and wooded edges such as Benthall and Wenlock make for superb rambles.

To Clun Forest

Returning to the south west of the county, it is in this part that the highest hills are to be found. The Long Mynd is well known to many and Caradoc, the Lawley, and Ragleth almost as well. But move west towards Clun Forest and this isolated sheep farming country offers a solitude rarely found elsewhere. A mile or so away from the 'honeypot' areas and you are off the beaten track, especially if you can get away on Saturdays or during the week. It is wild country.

Stay Awhile

These introductory comments offer no more than the briefest sketch, a whetting of the appetite to discover this delightful part of England. In such a short space it would be impossible to capture the unsophisticated charm of Shropshire country life exhibited in local farming, crafts, village events and town markets. Walking is not just about notching up mile after mile, it is about gaining a feeling for the landscape, staying awhile at a village inn, or local cafe, talking to people who live and work in the countryside. The visit becomes so much more enjoyable and especially if you stay for a night or two in the area where you are walking. You can relax and get to know a place more without rushing around in a car.

Shropshire's Other Attractions

Besides the countryside, Shropshire has a growing number of attractions from the internationally recognised Ironbridge Gorge Museum to the much loved Severn Valley Railway. There's also the Shrewsbury Quest where you can find out more about the fictional medieval monk, Brother Cadfael. To the north is

Hawksworth Park, Victorian gardens and monuments used in the filming of The Chronicles of Narnia screened on television in recent years.

In many respects there's nothing better than coming across a farm open day or village carnival when you are on your travels. Most of the walks start from a village or town and many of these locations have an attraction or two close by. In this way you can make a really good day out by combining a walk and a visit to a local place of interest.

Wayside Curiosities

On your travels look out for many of the wayside novelties, the whipping posts at Morville, the ferry at Hampton Loade, the milestones on the Shroppie canal or the mining relics at Snail Beach. A favourite is the water trough which used to stand behind the Craven Arms Hotel and now sits less ceremoniously on the main A49 road. It has the inscription: 'Be Kind and Merciful To Animals'. Very thoughtful, but the trough has been concreted over in recent years!

The Taste of Shropshire

Many farms are now far more concerned to produce local speciality products and Shropshire is no exception. Travel along the main A49 road between Shrewsbury and Whitchurch and you'll find Maynards' home cured bacon, for example, or in Whitchurch itself some exquisite farmhouse cheeses to take home. Unlike its neighbour, Herefordshire, Shropshire has never been a big producer of cider but it still retains a number of small scale independent breweries, Woods behind 'The Plough' at Wistanstow, 'The All Nations' at Madeley and 'The Fox and Hounds' at Stottesdon, Hobsons at Cleobury Mortimer, Salop at Shrewsbury, and Hanby at Wem all brew fine ale and long live the tradition!

Country Pubs

Everyone likes a country pub, and Shropshire has dozens of them. Many have survived in the most isolated places and others have retained a strong local village trade over the decades. Having tried many of those mentioned on route (for quality control purposes, of course!), it has been a pleasure to meet so many interested landlords and landladies.

Most pubs warmly welcome walkers, but times have changed and gone are many of the bars which were built to serve the farmer and labourer. In order to survive, country inns have moved more towards providing accommodation and serving food. Generally speaking, many have retained their character and charm, which makes a break for a pint and a ploughman's a real pleasure. Children are almost always welcome at lunchtimes and early evenings (if they are not the over boisterous type) and there is outdoor seating at most places for warmer weather.

Publicans tend to dislike boots, especially if muddy, heavy rucksacks in dangerous locations, people eating their own food and are in the main not able to accept dogs. These aspects are not too good for trade and they're in business to make a living.

Opening hours are always a problem and there is no consistent pattern. Lunchtime opening seems to have been extended to about 3 pm, depending on custom at most places, with earlier opening in Summer evenings. Saturday is a better day, with more pubs staying open throughout. Sunday lunchtime hours are generally maintained through until 3 pm.

Pubs do add to a country walk, so enjoy yourselves en route or at the end of a ramble.

Long Distance Paths

Shropshire is host to a number of long distance paths including The Severn Valley Way, The Shropshire Way and The Offa's Dyke Path and the latest path, The Mortimer Trail from Ludlow through to Kington in Herefordshire. Offa's Dyke is a favourite. Of its 142 miles some of the best stretches straddle Shropshire. From the small town of Montgomery in Powys to the border town of Knighton the path winds its way between Wales and Shropshire crossing The Kerry Ridgeway into the tranquil valley of the Unk and onto Churchtown and then Newcastle. Some of the finest earthworks are to be found between Newcastle and Knighton. The Shropshire Way offers a circular walk, with optional sections, around the County. The route is as varied as the county itself and traverses paths and bridleways throughout with very little road walking. It came into existence through the good work of a number of rambling groups including several local branches of the Ramblers' Association in consultation with the County Council. The 172 mile route can be either accomplished on a walking holiday or as a series of walks between towns and villages on the main loop.

The Mortimer Trail is an exquisite route through lands once ruled over by the Mortimer family, hence the name. The 30 mile route follows a series of ridges between Ludlow and Kington offering marvellous views and real seclusion. There's a morning bus out of Ludlow to Wigmore just before nine which allows you the best part of the day to walk the trail back.

Walks In Shropshire
There have in recent years been a number of local booklets and leaflets published which outline local walks. Some are out of print now but others such as The County Council's 'Walks In Shropshire' series are on sale in libraries and tourist information centres. Telford Development Corporation and The East Shropshire Group of the Ramblers' Association have also produced a series of local walks in and around Telford.

The Walks
There are 36 walks featuring most parts of Shropshire from the deepest rural enclaves the other side of Clun to back ways through settlements borne of early industrialisation. Inevitably, some sections have been written up in recent years as part of other walks but most of the rambles are new in the sense of not being written up in recent years. It was with the cooperation of Shropshire County Council's Rights of Way team that many of them have been included. Most of them are now well-walked.

Information
The walks are from three to eleven miles in length and vary from

easy going to fairly hard. They were checked again in preparation for this second edition and few problems were found. Essential information is supplied at the beginning of each walk. In this way, for example, you can decide whether you wish to go for an easy ramble, visit a pub, call in at an attraction, etc. On the other hand, if you are looking for a hard five to six hours walk then these are listed accordingly. The choice is yours.

Family Walks

Many of the walks are suitable for families with younger children. Take, for example, the walks along the Severn Valley or in the Wyre Forest. They are ideal for families seeking a short ramble and an opportunity to move onto a local attraction. In fact, most of the walks can be adapted as they have cut-off points allowing shorter rambles for little legs.

Travel

Many of the walks included are possible to achieve by public transport. Shropshire is not very well-served by buses and some places are extremely difficult to get to in a day. Sunday buses are particularly limited. Nevertheless, there are sufficient walks for non-car users to enjoy on Mondays to Saturdays. A small number of the walks are specifically written up to include a rail journey. For example, the Knighton to Bucknell walk uses the Heart of Wales line or the Wem to Yorton walk, the Shrewsbury to Crewe line. These linear walks, using local trains, make for a day out with a difference and can be walked on Summer Sundays.

Tourist Information Centres and libraries carry a certain amount of bus information, but the large files of timetables are difficult to get to grips with. The County Council, however, also provides a countywide bus information service, Shropshire Traveline, on (0345) 056785, Monday to Saturday, and this might be an easier approach.

Train Information is more readily available from your local station or Shrewsbury station. Telephone (01743) 364041.

Directions

The suggested walking times provided in the text are merely for guidance. If you like a vigorously paced walk then the times provided will be over generous, but if you are out to saunter then they'll not be far wrong. Virtually all of the walks involve climbing stiles of some description. Directions are given assuming your back is to the stile every time you cross a field boundary. The County Council often waymark stiles which is helpful without being intrusive.

Maps

The walks should be easy to follow simply by using the instructions in the book. Some readers will want, however, to use a map in conjunction with the book. The Ordnance Survey maps 1: 50,000 scale Landranger Maps covering the area are adequate but far better for walking are the green-covered Pathfinder 1: 25,000 scale maps. The relevant ones are listed for each walk. They can be helpful when studying the lie of the land, the field patterns, the direction of streams and so on.

The Landrangers are, however, excellent for finding your way around the county. The key maps required are:
Kidderminster and Wyre Forest – Sheet 138
Ludlow and Wenlock Edge – Sheet 137
Shrewsbury – Sheet 126
Stafford, Telford and surrounding area – Sheet 127

Changing Environment

It goes without saying that there will be change. After all, you'll be walking through a working landscape. Crops will be rotated, barns built and trees planted where grass was once sown. Sometimes walks become a little overgrown in certain sections, even when a number of us walk them throughout the year and a stick can come in useful on such occasions. It is likely that some paths and bridleways will be improved since they were first researched for this publication. In other instances, there might even be minor diversions and alterations to the route. Wherever possible these are usually signed and easy to follow back to the original route. I can only apologise for such things in advance but common sense, no doubt, will prevail when you are out on the route.

A few matters do concern people when they're out in the countryside especially when they are not used to walking in an area of mixed farming. People sometimes hesitate when they cross a stile and find that a crop has been planted and the path not reinstated. Rights of way are literally what they mean. You are entitled to walk without obstruction whether it be a crop or other impediment along the way. Thus, you should keep to that way and tread a path accordingly. That is the law.

Although the regulations allow some bulls in fields crossed by rights of ways it is best to walk as far away as possible to them. Cows can be a little frisky in winter months when they think you are bringing them food but generally do not cause concern. In areas of grazing, fields are sometimes cordoned off by low level electric fencing which gives a mild shock to animal and human alike so step over them gingerly!

Any serious obstructions, however, should be brought to the attention of the Rights of Way section at the County Council. It is only by our reporting such matters that we save other walkers from difficulties.

We sometimes forget though that it is a working countryside so expect to come across lanes which are sometimes used by herds of cows in wet weather and hence can become very muddy. In fact, most paths are likely to be wet in places after rain so it is better to wear stout footwear – boots or Wellingtons. It is also essential to carry rainwear. On the hills it is vital that you wear proper windproof and waterproof garments in case the weather turns. A small amount of food and a first aid kit, compass and torch can be tucked into a rucksack without any discomfort.

Shropshire is a splendid county with an increasing number of footpaths being improved so that we can enjoy it more than has been possible during the past two decades. This book introduces you to some of these walks. Shropshire is a most promising county for the walker!

1: Acton Burnell

Easy walking in a quiet part of Shropshire.

Distance: 3 miles (5km)

Allow: 1½ hours

Map: Pathfinder Sheet SJ 40/50 Dorrington and Cressage

How To Get There:
By Car: From Shrewsbury by way of the A49 to Bayston Hill, then left to Condover, another left and right turn to Frodesley. From there it is another left to Acton Burnell. Alternatively, travel on the A458 to Weeping Cross where you turn off right to Pitchford and Acton Burnell by way of Cantlop Bridge.
By Bus: There is an infrequent bus service from Shrewsbury.

Refreshment: There is a shop and tea room in the village.

Nearest Information Centre: The Square, Shrewsbury.
Telephone: (01743) 350761/2.

Start the walk from the access road to the ruins of Acton Burnell Castle. You can either walk back along the tarmac lane to the crossroads, then turn left and left again just beyond the restored cottages, or simply do as the locals do and go through the access gate in the corner of the wooded area by the castle to join the path which leads to the Ruckley Road.

Special Licence

The castle, now in the hands of English Heritage, is open to the public at any reasonable hour. It comes as something of a disappointment to those expecting a lumbering great fortification for Acton Burnell was never a real castle. This castle was built in the late 13th century, more as a residence than a fortress. The owner,

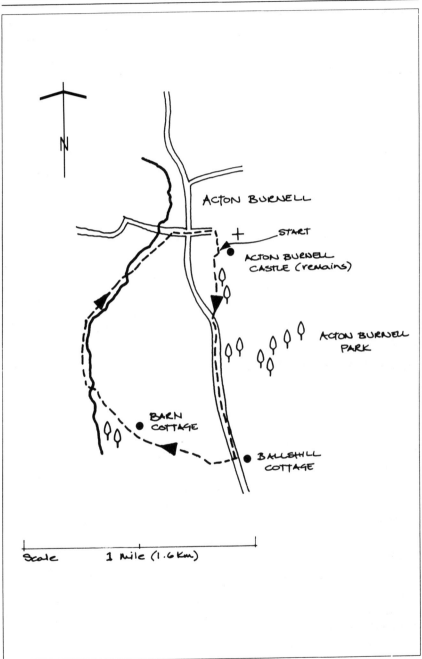

ACTON BURNELL

START

ACTON BURNELL
CASTLE (remains)

ACTON BURNELL
PARK

BARN
COTTAGE

BALLSHILL
COTTAGE

Scale   1 Mile (1.6 Km)

Robert Burnell – the Bishop of Bath and Wells, had to apply to the monarch for a special licence to make it look like a mock castle as in those days you required an early-day version of outline planning permission to do such things.

First Parliament

Behind the ruins of the castle stand two end gables of an earlier building referred to as 'The Parliamentary Barn'. It is thought that Edward I called a Parliament of sorts here to enact a piece of legislation to make notable debtors pay up to the monarchy within given time limits.

Acton Burnell Hall

Look further and you can see the elegant hall, now a college, with its grand Georgian frontage, a style of design much favoured by the affluent landowner of the 18th century. Do not miss the church, situated much closer to the castle, as it has some fine effigies of Sir Richard Lee and Sir Humphrey Lee, forefathers of Robert E Lee of the Wild West. Steal yourself away from these fine buildings for a while though on a short ramble in the Ruckley direction, with views over to Frodesley Lodge and The Lawley.

Acton Burnell Park

Once through the gate go left and continue alongside the wall boundary of Acton Burnell Park over stiles until you come out at a road. Go left and follow this road for a good half mile until you approach Ballshill Cottage on the left. Go through the gate on the right, opposite the access track on the left, and walk alongside the field boundary to your left into the next field by way of a gap in the hedge. Go slightly right, your landmark being the derelict Barn Cottage ahead. The stiles are missing here so go through the gateway and follow the fencing down to two gateways sitting virtually alongside. Go right through the second and then after a few paces cut across left now heading for a gateway to the left of the cottage.

Head for the left of the cottage and go gently right along a gorse bank before heading down the field with the wood to your left. Make your way to the far right-hand corner where you go through another gateway. Walk along the field's edge until you come to a bridge. Go over it and then turn right, following the stream into the shallow valley, offering the gentlest of landscapes. Cross an awkward stile of sorts and continue downstream through fields. You eventually come to a footbridge. Cross it and go left following the hedge to the barred gate. Go through it and bear slightly right through a gateway into the next field. Continue in this direction towards the stiles at the corner of the garden thus allowing access back onto the road in the village.

What a pleasant interlude in a quiet Shropshire valley, not changed much since those early Parliamentary days.

2: Aston-on-Clun

A delightful walk along paths and bridleways through a gently undulating landscape with fine views of Hopesay.

Distance: 3 miles (4.5km)

Allow: More than an hour

Map: Pathfinder Sheet 930 SO 28/38 Bishop's Castle and Clun

How To Get There:
By Car: Aston-on-Clun is on the B4368 between Craven Arms and Clun. Parking is very limited in the central part of the village.
By Bus: There is a limited service between Ludlow, Craven Arms and Aston-on-Clun.

Refreshment: The Kangaroo Inn at Aston-on-Clun.

Nearest Information Centre: County Branch Library, Church Stretton. Telephone: (01694) 723133.

Aston-on-Clun is a curious place. No only does it have a pub called The Kangaroo Inn (and there cannot be too many of those about) but it also has two stone built circular houses. Even more intriguing is the 'Arbor Tree', which is to this day decorated with flags to commemorate the marriage of local Squire Marston of Oaker to Mary Carter of Sibdon Carwood on Arbor day, 29 May, 1786. It sounds so romantic and to help the annual event along a bit the couple set aside monies for the villagers to festoon the tree on a yearly basis.

Decorating Trees

Ceremonies of a similar nature were commonplace a century earlier when trees were decorated at the command of King Charles II to celebrate the restoration of the monarchy on 29 May, 1660.

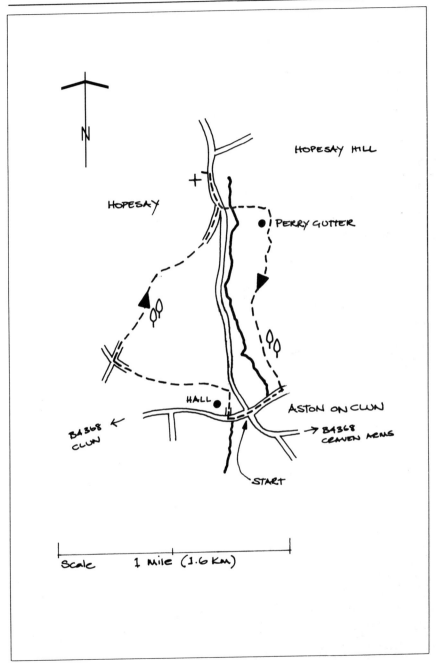

N

HOPESAY HILL

HOPESAY

● PERRY GUTTER

HALL ●

ASTON ON CLUN

B4368 ←
CLUN

→ B4368
CRAVEN ARMS

START

Scale   1 Mile (1.6 Km)

Very few such ceremonies have survived into the twentieth century the most colourful being the garlanding at Castleton in Derbyshire.

Start your walk from the Arbor Tree. Walk ahead towards Clun passing the Malt House to the left and the hall to your right. Just beyond, turn right along track which actually runs by the hall. At a crossroads go left and this eventually leads to a barred gate which you go through. The track becomes less distinct, greener, and with heavier undergrowth in places. A tree lined path leads to a wicket gate.

Go right here along a sunken track of some antiquity. Ignore the stile on the left. Simply follow the old lane up the valley, a classic country walk rich in wildlife. Follow the track for about a mile through to Hopesay. It rises up to a summit and through a gate, then proceeds through a bridlegate. There are barns to the left and you follow the path as it drops down and curves right. It becomes a clearer farm track which descends to a road.

Go left into Hopesay and left again up to the church, a blissful place in this quietest of corners. The church dates from Norman times and has an attractive Norman arched doorway. Nearby are several distinctive houses including the old rectory.

Hopesay Hill

Retrace your steps back to the junction at the southern edge of the hamlet where you entered previously passing the entrance to Fairmead. Within a matter of 20 paces beyond, go through a delightful iron kissing gate on the left. Walk ahead by the hedge on the left, cross the bridge and head slightly left to cross a stile. Continue ahead uphill towards Hopesay Hill moorland owned by The National Trust.

Look back over Hopesay before going through another iron gate. It is easy to see now why the settlement grew up in this particular part of the valley, at a meeting of brooks and sheltered by Aston, Burrow and Hopesay hills. It is pretty at all times but the colours of the woodland are at their best on a frosty Autumn morning when the sun is climbing over Aston into the valley. If you wish to climb

Hopesay Church

Hopesay Hill then head slightly left up a steep path to the summit. Take a breather and then retrace your steps.

Perry Gutter

Otherwise, go right and pass considerately by a dwelling at Perry Gutter to a stile and road. Evidently, this was a small hamlet in its own right in earlier times but, as with so many places in Shropshire, there has been a significant decline in population during the past century and, in some instances, even earlier.

Cross the road and go through another small gate, often tied with string, to climb up the bank. Continue ahead over undulating territory and the path begins to fall to the right of the conifers, where you will find a stile. Cross it and continue ahead into brambles and gorse until you come to a point where the field edge drops to the right. You continue ahead, however, and the path becomes a green track which sweeps through bracken into the next field. Keep ahead beneath a wooded area and then proceed to the barred gate with dwellings nearby.

Go right and the road leads into the village, passing by one of the round houses mentioned earlier, back to the decorated tree.

3: Bishop's Castle

A delightful short ramble for those wishing to walk off a lunch served in one of Bishop's Castle's fine hostelries. Easy walking with more downhill sections than climbs! Can be muddy in places.

Distance: 3½ miles (5.5Km)

Allow: 2 hours

Map: Pathfinder 930 SO 28/38 Bishop's Castle and Clun

How To Get There:
By Car: Bishop's Castle is just off the A488 from Shrewsbury or the A489 from Craven Arms. There is a public car park near to the livestock market in Station Street.
By Bus: There is a daily service from Shrewsbury and a less frequent service from Ludlow and Craven Arms.

Refreshment: There are inns, cafes and shops offering refreshment in Bishop's Castle.

Nearest Information Centre: Old Time, 29 High Street, Bishop's Castle. Telephone: (01588) 638467.

The excellent Civic Society Town Trail booklet invites you to look down High Street from The Market Square and imagine the town in earlier times, for Bishop's Castle retains a layout dreamed up in the twelfth century. The castle once stood at the top of the town, behind where The Castle Hotel is now situated and looked over a main thoroughfare running down to the church. A series of much smaller lanes crosses this main street to complete the grid.

The Three Tuns

While standing in this vicinity take a look down Salop Street at the

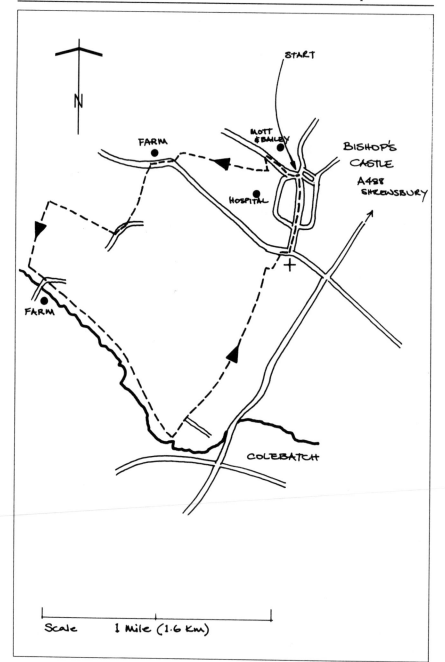

Three Tuns brewery and public house, dating from times when most public houses brewed their own. Until recently this sturdy survivor has lived through the recent decades of large scale brewery mergers, a miracle in times of a flood of global lager products. At the time of going to press the brewery had been closed pending a sale, hopefully.

A Rotten Place

Bishop's Castle has always been a significant borderland township, with markets attracting both English and Welsh over the centuries. It was at one time the smallest borough in England, known as a Rotten Borough in that its limited population did not really warrant two members of Parliament. Ironically, in 1820 all four candidates in the election polled a mere 87 votes each and in the absence of any other procedure they were all duly elected! From 1832 onwards the political status of Bishop's Castle has declined considerably.

Train to Nowhere

Of all the Shropshire lines the Bishop's Castle railway must surely have been the most loved. Built in the 1860s this railway was doomed from the beginning. The hopes of driving a road through to Montgomery and into Mid Wales were never realised and a track from Craven Arms to Bishop's Castle could never make commercial sense. Of its 70 years' existence, 69 of them were in the hands of the receiver! There are dozens of yarns about the line and even to this day older residents refer to it with great affection.

Bishop's Castle is a good place to stay for a few days. Pick up the Town Trail and Town Guide, combined with a few walks from this book and you have the makings of a superb mini break.

House On Crutches

Start from outside the Castle Hotel, looking downhill, and turn right into the Market Square, a small one at that, and on your left is the fascinating seventeenth century House on Crutches. Continue along Welsh Street, appropriately enough, towards Wales. The chances are that this was one of the key routes leading to the

Kerry Ridgeway, a main artery between the two countries in previous centuries.

On the right, to the rear of the Castle Hotel are the scant remains of the motte and bailey castle, as heralded in the town's name. Pass by modern houses on the left and a bungalow on the right. Go left through a kissing gate into a field. Continue slightly left by a ditch. As you approach houses turn right to walk to a stile midfield and onto another to the right of a barred gate. Proceed ahead, once again, to another stile, this time to the left of a barred gate and press on up mid-field at first but then slightly left up the bank by the trees and onto a stile in the top far left-hand corner of the field.

Kerry Lane

This leads to a road. Walk up to the corner, with an old farm, Caeglas, to the right and your way is through the gate on the left. This can get extremely wet at times so choose your steps daintily or you could end up with a covering of manure. At first, keep to the field boundary on the left but, as this falls away continue ahead to a gateway, the left one of the two. Go slightly left to meet another hedge and continue ahead with it on your right to the next stile. Cross this and you come to a small wood. Go through here to a road.

Colebatch

Turn right, but within a very short distance you bear second right by an enclosure used for sawing wood. Keep company with the hedge on the left as you begin to climb up to a stile. Cross it and continue uphill but as the gradient eases and you see a barred gate ahead go left through the barred gate on your left. What a view below as this path drops into Colebatch. This is very much sheep farming territory and the isolated farms are dotted on the hillside opposite.

Once at the stream turn left and take a walk in the downstream direction, through gates to the road and bridge. The shortest way back is to turn left, following the lane back to Bishop's Castle. If you'd like a walk in a very tranquil valley continue ahead with your first stile of many to cross in this section. Go through the first very long field across a number of stile ahead. In the next short field go through the gate on the right and follow the field hedge ahead again. Cross a stile into the next field and then ahead through another pasture to cross a further stile. You should come to a point at the end of a longer meadow beneath a bank of mixed woodland where you see a gate and stile on your right. Do not go through them. Instead go left up the hillside passing by the old quarry scar to the left to the field corner where you cross the stile.

Return to The Church

Your return section is straightforward. Simply continue ahead through the fields with the hedge to the right until you reach a track. Ignore the track rising left after a blue gate. Your track descends to a stile by a gate and then ahead by a number of houses on the outskirts of town. It curves to the right and then left before reaching a lane by the church. Go right and then left into the main street.

4: Bucknell and Knighton

A moderate walk with one steep climb out of Stowe hamlet up to Holloway Rocks. This is a linear walk between the railway stations of Knighton and Bucknell offering superb scenery in borderland country.

Distance: 7-8 miles (11-13km)

Allow: 4 hours

Map: Pathfinder Sheet S0 27/37 Knighton (Powys) and Brampton Bryan

How To Get There:
By Car: Bucknell is on the B4367 from Craven Arms to Knighton. It is also a mile off the A4113 from Ludlow to Knighton. There is a reasonable amount of on-street car parking in the village. Catch the train to Knighton for the start of the walk.
By Train: Knighton and Bucknell are stations on the Heart of Wales line. There are four trains each way on a Monday to Saturday, with a limited service on Summer Sundays. There is also a limited bus service on Monday to Saturday.

Refreshment: There are cafes and pubs in Knighton and two pubs and at least two shops in Bucknell.

Nearest Information Centre: Offa's Dyke Heritage Centre, Knighton or Castle Street, Ludlow. Telephone: (01584) 875053.

Arrive in Bucknell in time for the train or bus ride to Knighton. It is only a short ride away. The walk commences from Knighton station which happens to be just in Wales. This interesting borderland town, however, is well worth exploration. Known by the Welsh as Tref-y-Clawdd, meaning the 'Town of the Dyke', Knighton is the only settlement of any size actually situated on the dyke

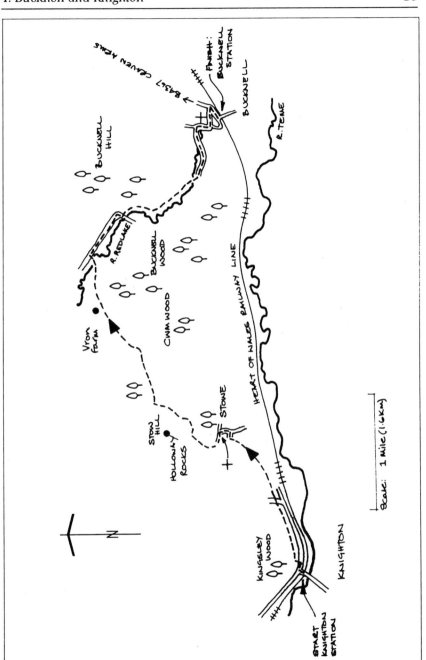

Scale: 1 Mile (1·6 Km)

itself. The path cuts through the town and beneath the archway by the Knighton Hotel.

Knighton is very much a market town and Thursday is the busiest day for the traditional shops huddled around the market place and dominant Victorian Clock Tower. It is two minutes walk from the unmanned station.

Kinsley Wood

From the station entrance turn right and once over the railway bridge turn right again. Walk along the main A488 road but only for a very short stretch before going left along a track which slopes upwards into the mixed woodland rich in ash, beech and oak. Follow this delightful path through the wood until you reach a forestry road with a sign indicating Kinsley Wood. At the other side of the U bend there are steps down to a stile beneath a tree. Cross it and your way is across the field, slightly left, to a stile leading onto the main A488. The stile is the landmark to head for but you have to cross a footbridge immediately beforehand. This cannot be seen until you are some way over the field.

Old Road to Stowe

Cross the road and go through the gateway. Continue ahead with the hedge to your left to the next gateway. Go through this and you are now walking through pleasant fields with the hedge to your right. It is hard to believe that this was once an old roadway to Stowe as it has long since lost its significance. The route is easy to follow through a succession of fields, always keeping the hedge to your right. The path begins to rise and if you look over your shoulder there's an impressive view of Knighton, sitting solidly on the banks of the Teme in the gap between Ffridd and Panpunton hills. It is easy to see from here why it was a such a fought over strategic gap town. The path leads up to a barred gate situated on a brow above Stowe. There is a superb view of the hamlet and Holloway Rocks beyond.

Stowe Church

At this point, your way should be left through the gateway then right across the fence downhill to the track below by the cottages. As there is no proper stile over the fence, most ramblers simply descend the hill. Once on the track below go right and then at the lane turn left, not immediately left, but to walk up by the church. This neat little church contains lovely stained glass windows, suggested by Nicholas Pevsner as being 'art nouveau' in style.

Holloway Rocks

Just beyond the church go left along a gated track which curves to the right as it climbs up a dry valley to Holloway Rocks, a niche in the outcrop of Stow Hill, a route which has no doubt given many a drover a hard time in bad weather. Rest awhile at the top for the views up the Teme valley are splendidly rewarding. Continue slightly left across the large and open field, beyond a pool to a stile which leads onto a forestry track.

Once on the track turn right and continue ahead until the corner of the plantation where the forestry track dips left. Your way should be straight ahead but movement of the boundary fences mean that ramblers now go ahead through two large gates and along the track with the fence to your left. Go through the gateposts and continue downhill. Again, the map shows a path cutting off to the left but walkers now continue to the next gateway and once through go left and pass through another gateway before joining a much clearer track which begins to descend towards Vron farm.

Another Caer Caradoc

There are good views of the Redlake Valley and exceptional view of Caer Caradoc, a relatively small Iron Age camp but at over 1200 feet, providing a strong defensive position. Could this have been the site of Caracticus's last brave stand against the Romans before his capture? Some say the event might have taken place at the fort on nearby Coxall Knoll. It is possible but most favour Caer Caradoc, near Church Stretton. You'll also see below the camp the hamlet of Chapel Lawn, literally meaning a clearing in the wood where a chapel can be found.

Follow the track down to the farm, then continue into a green sunken lane ahead. This descends to a group of farm buildings and by a bungalow to the River Redlake and to a lane beyond. Go right here and follow the road to a point just before the bridge. Go through the gateway on the left and follow the river bank to a stile in the field boundary. In the next field go left up the bank as the river meanders to the right, with dippers to be seen along this stretch. Cross the stile and join a more prominent path in the wood. Go right along this lovely green track which is easy to follow.

Bucknell

You come to the outskirts of Bucknell where the track meets a lane. Continue ahead through the gateway and this leads to a ford and bridge across the River Redlake. Cross the bridge and once on the road go left. Follow this through the sizeable village, passing by a public house and then right up to the church. Go left by the churchyard and at the next road junction go right by the Sitwell Arms to the railway station.

5: Buttonoak

Easy walking along woodland paths

Distance: 3 miles (4.8km)

Allow: 1 hour

Map: Pathfinder SO 67/77 Wyre Forest and Cleobury Mortimer

How To Get There:
By Car: Buttonoak is on the B4363 from Bridgnorth to Bewdley which joins the B4194. If coming in this direction the lay- by, which is not signed, is on the right after the Earnwood lay-by. Coming from Bewdley it is the first lay-by off to the left after Buttonoak hamlet.
By Bus: There is a regular service between Bridgnorth and Bewdley.

Refreshment: 'Button Oak' or New Inn public houses.

Nearest Information Centre: The Library, Bridgnorth. Telephone: (01746) 763358.

The Wyre Forest, in the far south east of the county, is one of the few remaining Royal Hunting Forests to have survived as a large area of traditional woodland rather than simply a name referring to a previous land use. Evidently, the Forest was well used by royalty during the Plantagenet and Tudor periods.

Part of the forest is a National Nature Reserve designated by the Nature Conservancy Council with a view to conserving it as a good example of native woodland rich in wildlife. The reserve is mainly based around the Dowles brook, which is also the county boundary.

There's a visitor centre at Callow Hill, in Hereford and Worcester on the A456 road between Bewdley and Tenbury Wells. There are also pleasant walks around Hawkbatch, closer to Bewdley.

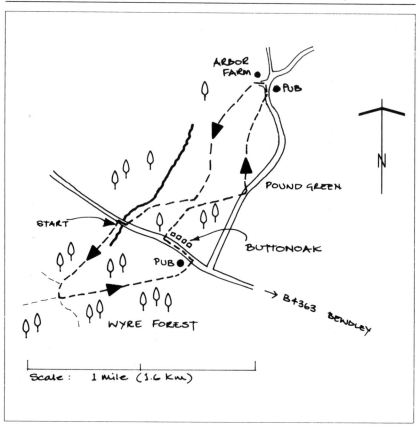

Start at the lay-by indicated above. The walk follows a number of paths and tracks over Forestry Commission land many of which are not dedicated as rights of way, so you will not be able to pick them out easily on your Pathfinder map. The Forestry Commission, however, welcomes considerate walkers and most paths are easy to follow.

Tunnel Vision

Follow the bridle path into the wood, which is deciduous at first then coniferous as you approach the summit after a gentle climb. At the first main junction go left, and in a short while, you come to a long linear grass clearing. Go left here and follow this towards

Buttonoak. It provides an unusual view. Is this what they mean by tunnel vision? The green passage begins to descend to a field. Go over the stile and follow the hedge on the left by the Button Oak public house. You come out onto the main road where you should cross and go left. In a short while you turn right to pass by forestry cottages to enter the woodland once again.

Delightful Woodland

About 20 metres beyond the houses the track forks. Keep right and you soon reach a shed. The path continues ahead through the wood to another junction where you keep ahead once again. At the crossroads go right and then cross a stile. Walk onto a drive past a house and to the green at Pound Green. Go slightly right over the green to the road junction and then bear left.

Take the first turn left, passing by Penny Cottage and follow the track as it runs by houses. It also passes bungalows and begins to curve left. You, however, keep ahead here. At the junction bear right. The path becomes a main track and leads up to the road. Go left to the New Inn public house.

Just beyond you go left to pass to the left of Arbor Farm. The track begins to curve left and you pass a stone cottage. The track bends right and you go left at the fork onto a lesser track which runs through high bracken. You meet another track and pass by a small building and a delightful orchard to your right. Keep ahead at the junction and walk through swathes of bracken again. You soon reach a main track. Go left.

Pass by a dwelling, Cherry Trees, on your left and go next right on a path leading to a stile by the wood. Head slightly right here until you reach a junction. Go right and then cross a main track. Keep ahead and cross another track. Cross two more paths and proceed in a similar direction. You now reach a stile into a small enclosure and go considerately through what is an outer garden of the cottage to the left where you will see rustic garden furniture for sale. On the main road turn right for the car park.

6: Cardington and Church Stretton

A longer ramble with several climbs. Mainly over paths and tracks. Splendid views.

Distance: 11 miles (18km)

Allow: 5-6 hours

Map: Pathfinder Sheet SO 49/59 Church Stretton

How To Get There:
By Car: Church Stretton is on the A49 between Shrewsbury and Ludlow. There is a car park off Sandford Avenue.
By Train: There is a daily service from Shrewsbury, Ludlow and beyond.

Refreshment: There are a number of inns, cafes and shops in Church Stretton. There is also The Royal Oak at Cardington.

Nearest Information Centre: County Branch Library, Church Stretton. Telephone: (01694) 723133.

Of the walking areas in Shropshire this must be an all-time favourite. Not only do the dinosaur edges of Caradoc and Lawley bring a sense of awe but the surrounding hills of Hope Bowdler, Helmeth and Willstone have an equal fascination.

Church Stretton is an engaging little town, which retains its spa influence as well as being a market place for the locality. In fact, it became something of a resort in the last century and one of the large supermarket chains is still supplied with mineral water from nearby Cwm Dale. In its heyday, however, at least one historian has pointed to the fact that water was brought up from Llandrindod Wells by train! It is a busy centre with a mix of accommodation and other facilities

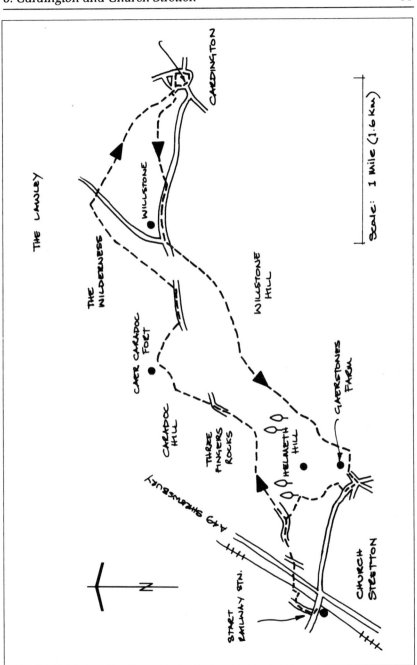

suitable for a few days stay. More importantly, the air always feels just right for walking.

Start at the railway station. Leave from the 'Shrewsbury trains' platform, and walk up the access road to Sandford Avenue. Cross over to join Essex Road which you walk along. Opposite the new houses go right, as signed, along a path which passes by sheltered accommodation and then crosses the railway lines. Do be vigilant. Continue to the main A49 road and be even more vigilant as you cross.

Old Roman Road

On the other side use the link path ahead to a back lane, the old Roman Road, which you cross and go over a stile into a field where you can see bungalows to your right. The path leads left up to a stile. Cross this to join a road. Bear left and after the old sunken road on the right go right over the stile and along the field boundary adjacent to the old road on your right.

Follow this to the gateway in the upper corner of the field and walk up the muddy track. Keep to this track at first then, after 150-200 metres cross the stream on the left by a footbridge and then the well-worn path which climbs up to a more prominent track. Follow this up the hillside until it bends right. You go left over a prominent stile between hawthorn and hazel on the left. A well-worn path leads up to Caradoc, a very steep climb which will set the heart pacing.

Caradoc

Here are the remains of an Iron Age hill fort standing on Shropshire's most impressive ridge. It is no surprise that this site is also thought to have been Caracticus' last battle with the Romans, with at least two other contenders. With the Roman Road being so close and the hill fort being such a dramatic site you could well imagine it. In fact, on a clear day it is easy to stay and dream here for most of the day but there's walking to be done.

By all means walk up to the summit for the views, including an excellent one of Cardington church and village to your right.

However, your way is to take the green path which descends to the right before the main outcrop. There's a good view of the Lawley ahead and the ridge known as the Wilderness to the right in the foreground. Cross a stile then proceed across a field, level at first then a sharp dip down the bank to cross a stile and a track where you go left.

The Wilderness

The track drops and then climbs gently to a stile by a gate on the left. Go this way to walk along a slight ridge known as the Wilderness. Head slightly right across the moor. Cross a stile by a barred gate and proceed ahead. You pass through old workings and cross another stile. Keep ahead, ie ignore the stile on the right and you soon reach a stile by a gate. Follow the track down to a road.

Cross the road and the stile. Keep company with the hedge to the right until the next stile then after a short distance the path crosses a stile and leads left with the hedge now to your left. Cross two further stiles ahead and, as you come closer to Cardington village, go through a stile at the bottom right corner of a tapered field and continue with a hedge to your left. This leads to a track which takes you into the village.

Cardington

Turn left and then choose either fork of the village triangle to the Royal Oak. The village is a fine collection of traditional stone and half-timbered buildings huddled together around the church. The latter dates partly from Norman times and has a number of interesting aspects including a splendid effigy of Judge William Leighton, one time resident in nearby Plaish Hall where rumour has it that the elaborate chimneys were built by a condemned convict in the hope of receiving a pardon. He hanged nevertheless, some say from the very same chimneys, which doesn't say much for the kindly old judge – but after all it is legend.

Retrace your steps to the lane where you first entered Cardington. Go down it but turn left before a gate. The track bends right to the fields, passing by a plantation. Cross the stile and go right up a narrow field strip, heading for the far left corner. Just before there is a stile on the left. Cross it and go right keeping the hedge to your right. Cross the next stile and go left. Come to two stiles guarding a footbridge and, once over, head slightly left up the field to another stile. Go slightly left up the field to a stile.

Willstone Hill

Go right along the road to pass by Willstone Farm. At the junction go left and then left again over a stile by a barred gate. Go ahead, mid-field, and along a tractor track passing through a gateway with Willstone Hill, and the Battle Stones, towering above you. The track ahead leads into the next field but beforehand go left by wire fencing along a less well-defined path to pass a pool. Cross a stile into rough pasture. Go slightly left up the hillside to a stile leading into bracken. Then, turn right on a track and after about 20 metres go next left up to a gate. Continue ahead, keeping near to the hedge on the right. Cross a stile and continue ahead through bracken. You reach a meeting of paths by a bridlegate. Keep ahead on a path which is not too clear on the ground. It continues ahead and leads up left to meet another path coming in from the left.

Helmeth Wood

Keep ahead, skirting the lower banks of Willstone, passing near to the ruins of a farm. Beyond is Helmeth Hill Wood, owned by the Woodland Trust, which is rich in wildlife. Look out for buzzards here. The path becomes less distinct, passing by several enclosures to the right. It eventually leads to a gate before the corner of a field, with Gaerstones Farm beneath you to the right.

Go through the gate and walk down to the stile by a barred gate. Cross this and go left along Hazler Road to the main road. Go right and as the road bends left you go right over the stile. Follow the field boundary to the left but ignore the bridlegate on the left leading into the paddock. Cross a stile and go right now up to the Woodland Trust entrance to Helmeth Wood. Follow the boundary down, on the left, to Cwm's Lane as waymarked.

From here retrace your steps into Church Stretton.

7: Caynham

A short ramble to Caynham Iron Age Camp

Distance: 3 miles (4.5Km)

Allow: 1 hour

Map: Pathfinder Sheet SO 47/67 Ludlow

How To Get There:
By Car: Caynham is signed from the Ludlow by-pass on the A49 or from Cleehill off the A4117 road from Bewdley. There is a limited amount of car parking by the telephone kiosk in the village.
By Bus: Twice weekly service from Ludlow.

Refreshment: Plentiful supply of cafes, shops and inns in Ludlow.

Nearest Information Centre: Castle St, Ludlow. Telephone: (01584) 875053.

No wonder A.E.Houseman had his ashes brought back to Ludlow church for it is one of the loveliest places in The Marches. It is very fashionable place to live these days and quite rightly so. Indeed it has been a sought-after place since the wool days when fortunes were made out of the sale of fleeces by diligent merchants.

Ludlow

Take a look at the town from any direction and you cannot fail to notice the prominence of the castle, particularly when arriving by train from the Hereford direction. This Norman fortress has withstood the ravages of time well; it is open to the public and is a centre piece during the lively annual Ludlow Festival.

Narrow medieval passages radiate from this quarter and yet close by there are many fine examples of Georgian architecture. Needless to say, there are a dozen guide books to sing the praises of Ludlow and virtually all of the walks from the town are written up in either the Shropshire Walks leaflet or other publications so why not try them? Add this little ramble to the itinerary and you have the makings of a good weekend. You cannot do justice to Ludlow in less time.

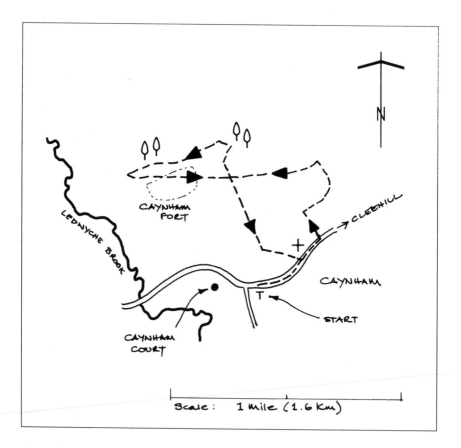

Caynham

Caynham is a traditional hamlet which has had an increase in housing during recent years. It has a number of interesting features including the school which was the first National Society school to be built in Shropshire sometime in 1834, a date which can still be seen above the door.

Site of the Village Pound

Just down the road is an unusual plate which marks the site of the village pound, an enclosure for stray animals. The small green in the centre of the village is very pleasant.

Start the walk from the telephone kiosk in the village and turn right. Walk the short distance up to the church and pass the churchyard with its yew trees and ancient cross. You will see these on the return leg.

Continue along the road. Pass by double gates and then go left over a stile as signposted. Go ahead to follow a line up the field towards a solitary tree and then up to a point parallel with a field corner on your right. It is at a point where the electric telegraph poles cross. Go right to walk to the field corner but just beyond is a stile beneath an old tree. Cross it. You will see the buildings of a farm to your right.

Head slightly left up to the top right corner. Cross the stiles beneath an oak and go right to follow the field's edge on the right.

In the top corner cross a stile tucked in between thick bushes. Keep ahead to a stile in the next fence and proceed in a similar direction towards the next stile. Do not cross it. You will be returning over it later. At this stage, go right to another stile which you cross and then curve around the edge of the small hollow around to a stile leading into the wood.

Cross this and walk down the track ahead where you go over another stile by a gate. As the track approaches the field, however, you go left along a narrower path, sometimes overgrown, through the wood, always keeping close to the field boundary on your right. Come out of the wood to a pasture and continue ahead towards a stile. Do not cross here for this is a junction of paths and you are changing tracks. Instead, turn around and go slightly right up the slope towards the hill fort ramparts. Do not be tempted to use the stile ahead leading into the wood but go right up a steep section of embankment.

Caynham Camp

At the summit you go left, as signed, across this ancient camp to a gap in the ramparts and to a stile adjacent to a gate. The camp is a very evident Iron Age site; the ramparts can be seen quite clearly surrounding its 8 acres.

Cross this stile and the next where you continue, slightly left, to meet the stile seen on your outward journey. Go over it and then turn right.

Descend the hillside to pass by an old scar and go through a gateway. You will see the old track on the left as you proceed through another gateway. By an old tree stump go left over a stile and head slightly right to the church. Go through the churchyard and exit onto the road. Go right to retrace your steps back to the start.

8: Cheswardine

Easy walking through a little known part of Shropshire, including a short section of tow-path along 'The Shroppie' canal.

Distance: 4-5 miles (6-8km)

Allow: 2 hours

Map: Pathfinder Sheet SJ 62/72 Hodnet and Norbury

How To Get There:
By Car: Cheswardine is signposted from the Main A529 road between Hinstock and Market Drayton. It is also accessible by way of Hales and Chipnall from the A53 route between Newcastle-under-Lyme and Market Drayton. There is limited on-street car parking in the village.
By Bus: The service to Cheswardine is very infrequent but Market Drayton is served by the X64 Shrewsbury to Hanley express bus and a walk along the Shropshire Union canal by way of Tyrley Locks makes for a lovely day's walking.

Refreshment: There are public houses in Cheswardine and Soudley in addition to a village store.

Nearest Information Centre: The Square, Shrewsbury.
Telephone: (01743) 350761.

Where West Staffordshire meets Shropshire, you'll find a delightful group of villages which epitomise rural England. Cheswardine is one of these, with its commanding church, village post office and inns within a stone's throw of the quiet road junction.

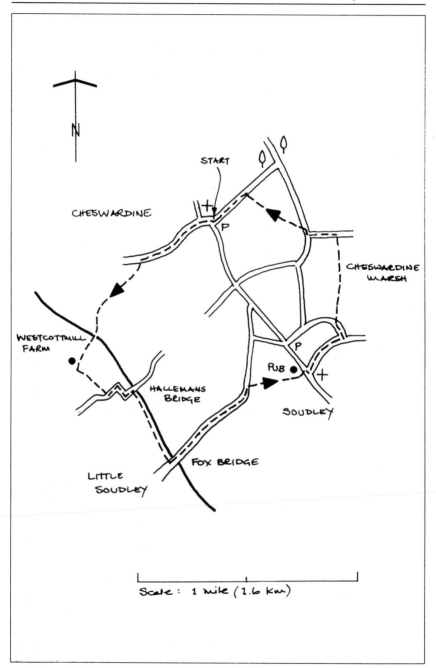

Scale: 1 mile (1.6 km)

Gingerbread Aphrodisiac

Cheswardine is just in Shropshire but this has not always been the case. It is mentioned as 'Ciseworde' in the Domesday Book and listed under Staffordshire. More than one writer suggests that the name is related to cheese making and dairying is still important in the area. Nearby Market Drayton sells itself, however, not on cheese making but gingerbread and a local Cheswardine baker still holds an original recipe. Some say that it definitely has aphrodisiac properties so stock up if you find some. Do take care not to eat too much before the walk!

Start by or from the 'Fox and Hounds' public house in the centre of the village. Walk up the slope to the junction by the church and then follow the road around to the left, signed to Market Drayton. The road sweeps away from the village and soon you come across a group of cottages on both sides of the road. Just before the ones situated on the left is a stile leading into the fields. Cross it and keep company with the hedge on your right.

The Shropshire Union Canal

You come to a stile by a small pond teeming with wildlife despite the thoughtless dumping of rubbish here. Go over this and again keep to the hedge on your right. Go through a barred gate ahead and proceed alongside a hedge which is predominantly holly. You come to two stiles. Cross both and bear slightly left across the field to a gateway mid-field, coming to a track which leads to a bridge over the Shropshire Union canal. You have a choice of route here. Most ramblers use a little link path to the right of the bridge down to the canal tow-path and then turn right along the canal-side. Otherwise, the path ahead follows the track around the fields edge (rather than cutting the corner as indicated on the path-finder) to the farm buildings. Again, most walkers follow the track between the buildings and then go left. This farm track leads to a tarmac lane and here you turn left. At the canal bridge, known as Hallemans Bridge, there is an access path down to the tow-path. Go right.

Soudley

Whichever route is chosen you continue along the tow-path, boats passing, until the next road bridge, Fox Bridge No.52 where you climb up to the road and go right. Walk along this quiet lane for half a mile and where it bends right and left look for a stile on the right which is crossed. The path follows the field edge on your right almost to the corner but then cuts across left to a stile. Cross this and walk slightly left towards the top left-hand corner of this next field where there is a stile by a gate leading onto a tarmac lane. To the left is the Wheatsheaf public house, and over the road is a Wesleyan chapel dated 1837.

Cheswardine Marsh

Cross the road and walk up the lane opposite. As this begins to dip down by an old truncated signpost go left onto a narrow lane. As this road begins to bend to the left, go right through a 5 barred gate. Keep close to the hedge on your right and walk down this long thin field to Cheswardine Marsh, not that it is very marshy now. Nevertheless, it can get wet, even though the farmer has gouged out a large drainage channel crossed by a sleeper bridge. Begin to walk slightly left away from the hedge to cross a stile. Continue ahead and cross the next stile to the right of an old tree stump. Go right to soon reach another stile. Go over it and then turn left to walk along the road.

Return to The Church

Pass by the road junction and the road veers right. There is a stile and signpost on your left. Cross the stile and go slightly right across the field, with Cheswardine church coming well into view. You should be aiming for a point just to the right of the church tower. The way is clear from here with a stile and an old gate to cross before reaching another stile leading into a lane. Go left and walk the short distance into Cheswardine village.

9: Chirbury

A pleasant short walk along paths with limited road sections. There are a few climbs.

Distance: 4 miles (6.5km)

Allow: 2 hours

Map: Pathfinder Sheet 909 SO 29/39 Montgomery

How To Get There:
By Car: Chirbury is on the B4386 between Shrewsbury and Montgomery or the A489 and A490 from Craven Arms.
By Bus: There is a daily, except Sundays, service to Chirbury from Shrewsbury but it is infrequent.

Refreshment: The public houses in Chirbury.

Nearest Information Centre: The Square, Shrewsbury.
Telephone: (01743) 50761/2.

Chirbury is on the road to Montgomery, a very small Welsh Georgian town which is overlooked by the impressive ruins of Montgomery castle. It might be worth combining a trip across the border to this superb little town and then call back into Chirbury for a refreshing ramble. On the other hand, Mitchell's Fold is but a few miles away, beyond the hamlet of Priest Weston. This Bronze Age stone circle has fifteen remaining uprights. It was probably a place of religious significance and also no doubt has been used for star gazing purposes. If travelling by car, be warned about the track up to the monument. You need a very sturdy exhaust system.

The village of Chirbury lies in unspoilt country. Its church is somewhat large for the size of the settlement but this perhaps can be explained in that it was once part of a thirteenth century priory. Remains can still be seen in the churchyard.

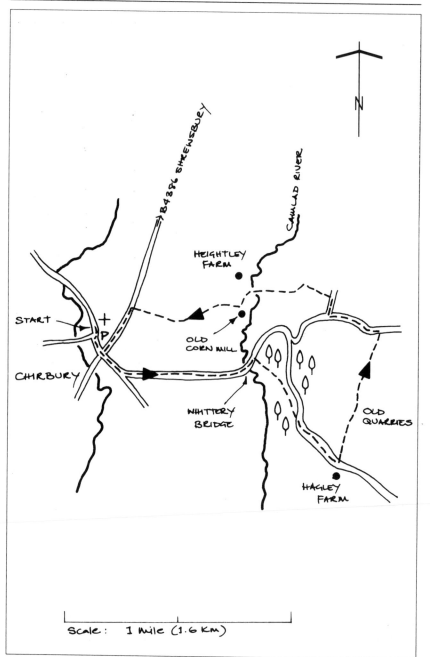

From the church go left and follow the main A490 road through the village towards Churchstoke but after a short distance take the left-hand turning to Whittery Bridge, a distance of about half a mile. There is also a beautiful walk along Marrington Dingle from here but on this occasion cross over the bridge over the Camlad River, the only river in West Shropshire to flow into Wales rather than England.

As the road begins to climb left bear right, after the gate, onto a narrow path hidden with summer brambles but which, after a few metres turns out to be a superb woodland path rising up slowly towards the remains of an old quarry. This leads to a stile which you cross and then make your way through a new plantation to a stile in the top right-hand corner of this plot.

Old Quarry Workings

Join the tarmac lane and go right, climbing once again, for a short while until you bear left opposite Hagley farm, not into the quarry, but to the left of this by the enclosure. Go through the gateway and continue to walk to the right of the old quarry workings beneath the bracken clad banks. This climbs up to rougher land where you head across to the barred gate. Continue ahead with a solitary tree on the right and hedge on the left to meet a lane.

Go left here and then right at the next junction. Follow the farm track towards the stream but before cross the stile on the left. Walk down to the stile in the bottom right-hand corner, cross it and then go slightly left to dip into the top of the dry valley. Go right but then left to skirt the shoulder of the hillside The path is not distinct on the ground but head for the bridge across the Camlad. The views of the valley are good from this vantage point.

Old Corn Mill

Once over, continue ahead over a sleeper bridge and then go left . You go left. You will see the remains of the old corn mill by the river. Doesn't it look forlorn? What a busy site this must have been centuries ago, with horse-drawn carts bringing corn from miles around.

Climb up the steep bank by the hawthorns to a point by an old tree stump and an electric telegraph pole. Cross the wooden fencing here into a field. Go slightly left across the field to a stile. The farm stands to your right. Cross the stile and then head slightly left to another stile almost equidistant between two oak trees in the next boundary hedge. Cross this, then head slightly left to cross a further stile. You now continue ahead by the hedge on the left to the B4386 road where you turn left for the village.

10: Chirk And Selattyn

The Ceiriog valley, Offa's Dyke and the Chirk aqueduct
make this walk to Selattyn varied and full of interest.
Several climbs and a few miles of road walking. Although
the walk begins and ends in Wales it is predominantly in
Shropshire. A torch is essential!

Distance: 10 miles (16 km)

Allow: 5-6 hours

Map: Pathfinder Sheet SJ 23/33

How To Get There:
By Car: Chirk is on the main A5 road from Shrewsbury. There is
on-street car parking near to the railway station.
By Train: There is a daily service from Shrewsbury and Chester.

Refreshment: There are cafes and inns in Chirk, Chirk Bank and The
Cross Keys at Selattyn.

Nearest Information Centre: Mile End Services, Oswestry.
Telephone: (01691) 662488.

Chirk is a small town in Clwyd and has a pleasant atmosphere
except for the drone of heavy vehicles in the main street. The Afon
Ceiriog cuts its way deeply here and the Chirk aqueduct and
railway viaduct look spectacular across the valley. Nearby is Chirk
Castle, a domesticated fortress set in magnificent grounds. Now
owned by The National Trust, it is open to the public throughout
the summer.

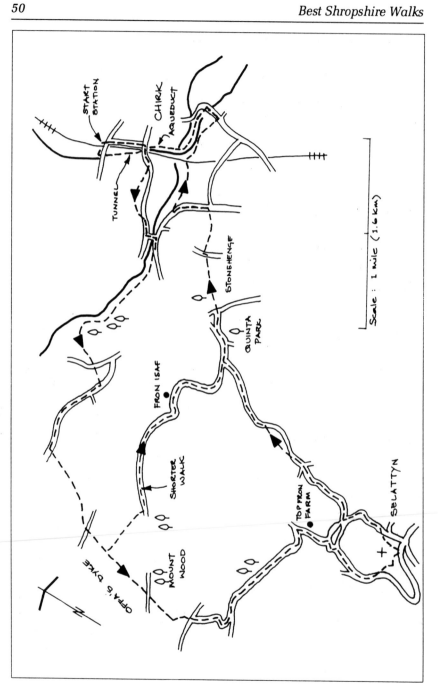

Wat's Dyke

This is a good place to pick up Offa's Dyke if you are considering a walking tour. Nearby is also the less well known and researched Wat's Dyke which ran from the Dee to Oswestry. Earthworks can be seen near Rhyn and closer to Gobowen and Oswestry. It obviously served a similar purpose to Offa's construction and is said to be older. Perhaps, Offa's men modelled their on this earlier dyke.

Start the walk from Chirk station, which, as mentioned previously, is in Wales! Cross the road and continue ahead with the railway cutting on your right. At the next junction go right. There's a good view of the aqueduct and viaduct from here. Pass by houses and go right through the barriers along a path which bears left and ahead. Ignore the right-hand turn but go left through a wall before the parkland of Chirk Castle. Descend to the road. Cross over and go right down to the bridge.

Afon Ceiriog

Go left over the bridge which spans the beautiful Afon Ceiriog into Shropshire and then turn right. Just after the telephone kiosk turn right to cross a stile by a gate, as signed, to the meadow alongside the river. The earth works here look very much as if there was a mill pool on this site. Follow the riverside to the stile leading into the woodland owned by the Woodland Trust. There has been a landslip in recent times so follow the diversion left.

This path dips then cuts immediately left and then right up the hillside. It eventually rises up a steep sided gully to steps which exit onto a road. Go left and then right at the junction after the entrance to the hall. The road rises up and bends right through a farm and over a bridge. It climbs once more and as it bends left keep ahead.

There are great views of Chirk castle from this track. This property contains a number of rather fine state rooms full of Adam style furniture and other artefacts from the past three centuries. Further up the Ceiriog Valley is Pontfadog and Glyn Ceiriog, villages of character in this beautiful part of the world.

Offa's Dyke

After about half a mile you come to Offa's Dyke Path. Walking parts
of the Dyke is always interesting as you can chew over in your mind
why it was built in the first place. Along certain sections it looks
very much like a defensive earthwork and in others as if it were
merely a prominent boundary to mark territory rather than for
military purposes. The latter explanation tends to be favoured by
historians and it was, no doubt, used to regulate trade between
Mercia and Wales.

Chirk Castle

Go left over the stile and follow the dyke along a very clear section
until you come to a tarmac lane which you cross. Take care on the
next bit as it drops very steeply into a ravine and there's an even
steeper climb out of it. Shortly afterwards you cross a bridleway
and for those requiring a shortened version of the walk this is a
useful cut off point. Go left along the bridleway (which can get
overgrown in places) to the road and then go left to a corner beyond
Fron Isaf. Here you pick up a path to Quinta where you rejoin the
longer walk.

Morlas Brook

Otherwise, for those seeking the full version keep ahead on the dyke coming to another lane which you cross with Mount Wood to your left. Continue until you come to a stile which crosses the dyke and you go ahead, away from the dyke, to the corner of the field where you cross another stile leading down-field to a lane. Go left to pass the entrance to Clawdd and within a few paces bear right down an old track which passes cottages and becomes a metaled road. It winds right and left over the Morlas brook, to the main road.

Go next left down the lane signed unsuitable for heavy vehicles. Follow this road for about half a mile until it curves left at a junction. You go right and right again at the junction with the drive to Top Fron Farm. Follow this old by-way down the hillside avoiding tracks off to the left or right until you come down to the house by the stream. Go right here and climb up to the main road.

Go left and, at the corner go left over a stile by a gate opposite an old farm and with a dwelling on the left. Follow the hedge down the field and then take the track leading off right down to the footbridge over the stream. Notice the stone bridge. Climb up by Selattyn church and then go left at the road towards the Cross Keys public house.

Selattyn

This old village is thought to have been a frontier trading post in more turbulent past centuries. There are certainly a large number of tracks leading into Selattyn and it is very much a crossroads to this day. The church is in an imposing setting. Legend has it that an early nobleman found a white hind on this site which led him to dedicate the land for religious purposes. Accordingly, he had an ancient church of Bryn Hen Eglwys removed to here. The church has been cherished throughout the centuries and the interior was beautifully restored during Victorian times.

If not staying awhile, go left before the pub (No Through Road) and go along a lane to a stile beyond new houses which are on the right. Cross it and follow the hedge around to a stile on the right.

Take care as this drops down to a lane where you turn left. Follow this down to Nant Isaf and then the road bends over a bridge and up to a junction. Keep right to walk uphill again. At the junction continue ahead and, as this lane begins to curve right, go left over a stile and then head slightly right across fields. You come to another stile in the corner of the field which you cross and continue diagonally ahead to a stile exiting by way of a sleeper bridge onto the lane once again.

Quinta

Go left here, right at the next junction, left at the next and right at the next. You see Quinta Park to your right with the elaborate Victorian house of the same name. The road comes to a fork. Go right beneath the bridge and at the next junction you cross the stile ahead with some relief, no doubt, onto parkland. You will see a folly looking like a miniature Stonehenge, one of many pieces of fine stonework throughout the parkland.

Stonehenge

Go directly ahead and cross the stile leading into the woodland. Ahead is an early pedestrian tunnel which you can avoid if you wish as you continue to the woods edge. Go ahead down the field to a barred gate by an electric telegraph pole. Once on the road go left, and after 20 metres, turn right through a pedestrian tunnel and up to a stile. Cross it and keep ahead with the hedge to the left. Come to a duet of stiles and cross the field to the left of the farm buildings to a stile beneath an ivy clad oak.

Cross the stile and go left along the lane. Beyond a house the lane drops and you go right along a track which climbs up through the woods to a stile. Cross this and go left to the railway. Cross the tracks with care and follow the field's edge to your left. At the last telegraph pole the path cuts off right to another pair of stiles which you cross and then go down to the kissing gate, into Chirk Bank.

Telford's Aqueduct

Go left, cross the canal bridge and go left again along the tow-path. This leads to the magnificent aqueduct engineered by Thomas Telford and there are great views from here. You will see the notice, that the Shropshire Union Canal Company allows walkers along the path 'on sufferance only'!

Light at the End of the Tunnel

At the other end is your chance to use your torch, for the tow-path leads through the Chirk tunnel to a cutting by the railway, where you turn right and climb up the bank to the station. If you do not fancy this last exciting stretch simply go right up the embankment before the tunnel and cross the road to retrace your steps to the starting point.

11: Claverley

Gentle walking in an area dominated by arable farming.
Partly across fields and along quiet back lanes.

Distance: 4 miles (6.5km)

Allow: One and a half hours

Map: Pathfinder Sheet 911 SO 69/79 Bridgnorth and Much Wenlock
and SO 89/99 Wolverhampton (South)

How To Get There:
By Car: Claverley is signed from the A454 Bridgnorth to Wolverhampton road. There is limited on-street parking in the village but
avoid the junction by the church as larger vehicles have difficulty
passing.
By Bus: There is a service Monday to Saturday from Wolverhampton.

Refreshment: Claverley is well-endowed with public houses and you
pass by the inn at Heathton.

Nearest Information Centre: Listley Street, Bridgnorth.
Telephone: (01746)763358.

Claverley has several half timbered buildings, rose-covered cottages and rustic looking inns settled on the slopes near to the
impressive looking church of All Saints. It really does look as pretty
as a picture. When restored at the turn of the century the parish-
ioners were astonished to find in the church medieval 'Bayeux
Tapestry' style wall paintings depicting battle scenes hidden since
the fifteenth century.

Notable Houses

The village has for some time now attracted visitors, although it is
mainly a dormitory area. There are several notable houses in the

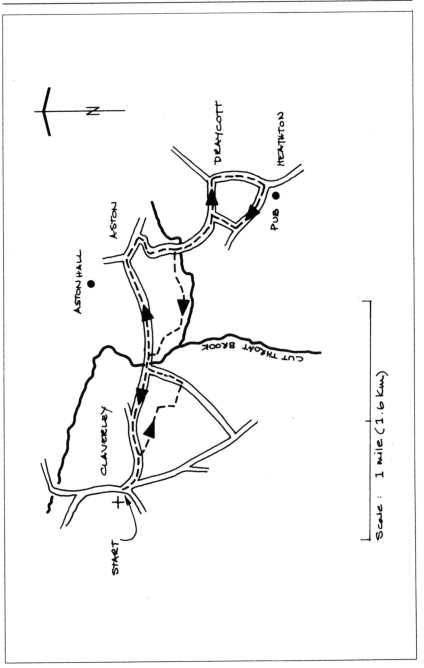

area including Chyknell and Ludstone. The main characteristics though, are the extensive tracts of arable farmland broken only by sandstone ridges and gentle brooks.

From the church, walk up the road by the three public houses and after the Plough you will see a telephone kiosk on the right. Go right here and then on the left is a path leading off over a stile into a small field. Go slightly right, cross the next stile and continue in the same direction to a barred gate. Go through and turn right along a green track. Follow this until it comes to a tarmac lane between a house and outbuildings.

Aston

Turn left here and walk the short distance to the next junction where you turn right. Follow the road, which is narrow in places, through arable farmland to the delightful hamlet of Aston with Aston Hall to your left. However, at the junction your way is right along a much quieter lane which passes by an old farm and then dips into a valley to a ford. Climb up to Draycott and go ahead at the first junction. Go right at the second and this brings you up to the Old Gate public house at Heathton.

The Old Gate

If not imbibing, turn right and follow the road for a short stretch to another junction where you turn right and then turn left at the next. You are now retracing your steps to the ford passed earlier. Look out for the stile on the left a few steps over the brook. Go left over it and the path rises up the bank closer to the hedge on your right. Follow this hedge eventually to the field corner by the wood. Below the stream meets another, affectionately named Cut Throat Brook, to flow towards Claverley.

Cross to the next field and walk along the boundary fence by the wood until you come to a stile allowing access to the road encountered on the outward journey. Go left and walk the half mile or so back into Claverley.

12: Clee St Margaret

A splendid walk over The Brown Clee to villages of considerable charm, along several paths and bridleways little used by the walker. There are a few steep climbs. A packed lunch is vital.

Distance: 10 miles (16km)

Allow: 5-6 hours

Map: Pathfinder sheets SO 68/78 Highley and SO 48/58 Craven Arms

How To Get There:
By Car: Travel on the B4364 between Ludlow and Bridgnorth. In Cleobury North village take the turning to Ditton Priors and then go left at the first junction. This road curves to the right and visitors usually park either side of the road near the information board at the Brown Clee Picnic Area and Forest Trail.
By Bus: Not accessible by bus. Limited service to Cleobury North from Ludlow.

Refreshment: There is a shop in Cleobury North. The nearest public house is at Ditton Priors, about a mile away.

Nearest Information Centre: Listley St, Bridgnorth. Telephone: (01746) 763358.

Brown Clee Hill, like Titterstone Clee has seen considerable economic activity during the past two centuries but is now a windswept moorland planted with woodland on the gentler eastern slopes. There is a real sense of isolation on the tops although there are telecommunications installations at certain places.

Start from the information board, which provides details about the forest trail in the Boyne Estate. Go through the stile by the gate and follow the path as it curves right to cross a stile then left in a

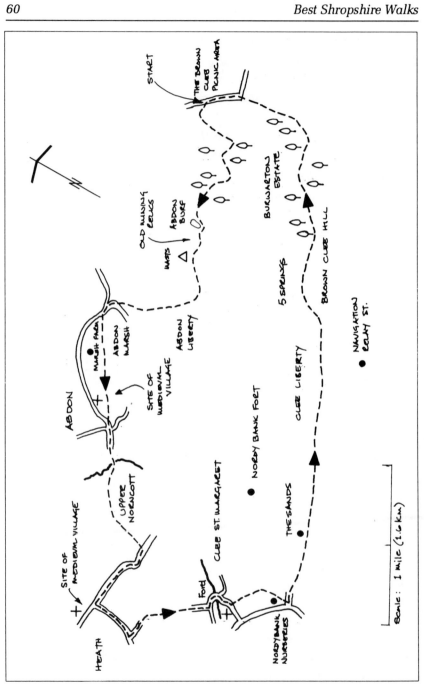

green swathe surrounded by jungle style bracken, to a point where you can see the cottages to your right.

Forest Trail

The path turns left here to 'Point 1', the start of the forest trail where you can buy a trail leaflet. Continue to climb up to the wood. At the main junction go left and after a short distance there's a stile and gate on the right. Go over it and follow the very clear path which climbs up through the wood curving left and then right up to another gate and stile.

Old Mine

Keep ahead to cross the track onto a tractor track ahead. This leads through a group of trees and then weaves its way up through marshy ground up to and to the left of a plantation of beeches. The path crosses a small stream and sweeps left as it breaks into rough ground with a scramble up exposed rocks.

The path climbs up to a point to the right of a pool and at this stage be able to see the remains of an old mine. The path remains indistinct but you can see your way ahead. Simply head for the left of the radio masts beyond.

Abdon Burf

These remains are one of the early mineral working and it is thought that the area has been mined for coal and other minerals for centuries but only on a small scale. Most of this ceased in the 1930s.

Although the Pathfinder map indicates that the right of way goes directly through the pool, go for a drier option and continue ahead over rough ground to the road. It is then easiest to follow this left and around to the triangulation point. This is the highest point, believe it or not, in Shropshire at 1772 feet (540m). From here, there are splendid views over the County towards Wales but also a most pleasing panorama in the foreground to Corvedale.

Your way down into this picture is to the left, winding across

the windswept moorland to the boundary fence. Over the moorland to the left is a memorial to servicemen of all countries killed
in air crashes on the Clees. You pass near to it on the return section.
The fence is a junction of paths and your way is over the stile and
down a slightly sunken track which curves around right to a barred
gate. Go through it and follow the track down a hillside known as
Abdon Liberty to a lane. Continue ahead down to the junction with
a telephone kiosk on the right. Go left here and in a short distance,
as the road bends to the right, go over the stile on the left.

Site of Medieval Village

Continue ahead, keeping to the fence to the left, until you come to
a stile in the corner of the field, where you can see Marsh Farm to
your right. Cross the stile and continue ahead as the boundary
hedges narrow before you. Cross the stile here and the temptation
is to follow the old sunken green lane, which gets very green with
vegetation in the summer. Follow a line to the right of the old track
and as it curves around to the left cut right across the field to a stile
in the corner. Cross it. You will see Abdon church to the right. Keep
in a similar direction and in the next field is the site of the medieval
village of Abdon. Shropshire has a number of these abandoned
village sites. This is a fairly large one and reflects clearly rural
depopulation in earlier centuries.

   Cut through ahead to a gate and in the next field go slightly right,
to the right of the electricity transmission pole towards the farm
beyond. To the right of it is a stile in the corner of the field, which
leads onto a lane. Turn left and at the junction continue ahead and
cross the stile between two gates. Continue down the field with an
old track to your left. You join this as it meets the path at the
footbridge over a stream.

   Once over climb up the bank and half way up go left over a stile.
Head slightly left up the hillside to the next boundary where you
cross a stile. Go right and then go through a gap in the fencing in
the next hedge. There's a barn to the left. Keep ahead to cross
another two stiles and small fields. Then walk through the scrub
into a field. Keep company with a hedge on the right to wooden

fencing by a gate. Go left along a track to the road where you turn right for Heath.

Heath

Beyond the crossroads on the right is a spartan Norman chapel. A key can be obtained to gain access. The area surrounding the chapel was once a village but has long since gone. It is surprising that the chapel has remained and even though the population is sparse in these parts services are still conducted throughout the year.

Return to the cross roads and go left through a gateway by the No Through Road. Head slightly left across the field to cross a stile in the hedge. Go right down the field to the next boundary where you cross a stile. Follow the hedge to your left and then just before the corner cut off right to walk downhill, with views of Clee St Margaret Church and Brown Clee. Be vigilant here, for once you have crossed a stile your way is to the left towards the bottom corner, between bushes, down to the stream which you cross. Go through the gateway and climb up the track.

Clee St Margaret

Head directly across the field to a gateway between the holly and hazel and continue along the wooded lane to a junction. Keep ahead and follow it to a road. Go left, and walk through the widest ford in Shropshire, up to the next junction where you turn right in the delightful hamlet of Clee St Margaret. Pass by the church and at the corner of the farm building cut off left up a lane and at the first junction your way right up the narrow track between tall hedges. You emerge near to the entrance of Nordybank nurseries, which specialises in growing herbs, native wild flowers and herbaceous border plants.

Turn left and left again at the corner. As this track leads away to the left to the Yeld, your way is upwards, to the right of a hedge, brushing through lush bracken. This bends right and then left again rising up above the enclosures. Join a more prominent tractor track which you cross and now bear slightly right up the hillside towards a hawthorn hedge. A green lane climbs up to grazing moorland.

Microwaved

Take a look back at those ancient field patterns below and over to the Principality in the distance. To the left is Nordy Bank, a small Iron Age camp which nevertheless still looks a formidable site. Walk up the green path by the fence and pass by an isolated cottage known as The Sands, with a warning to trespassers which looks at first as if they will be microwaved. On closer inspection, but not too close, you will see that it reads 'Microwired'. Your way is directly ahead through bracken but then keeping slightly left, across tracks, for about half a mile until you reach an access road leading up to the Navigational Relay Station on Clee Burf. This is not an easy section. You should aim to keep left of both telecommunications towers.

Go right on the road for a short distance, over the bridge spanning a small stream and then as it climbs to a corner you go slightly left here, rising slightly through the bracken with farms on the opposite side of the valley to your left. Follow this old track as it climbs along the valley's edge towards Five Springs. It becomes less distinct and wet in places but the direction is clear.

At the head of the valley, with the wood before you and a track coming in from the left across the moorland, keep left to a metal barred gate and then an iron gate between trees. Go through it and the track descends gently and becomes more prominent track made up with aggregate. A track joins from the left. Go through the gate and you will see a house on the right. There's a trickle of a stream ahead and a track leading off to the right just beyond. This is not well-marked. Go right here, along a green track through tall trees. This path leads down to a main cross track. Go over this into the parkland and keep slightly left to join a lane where you go left.

Follow it to a junction where you keep ahead for the short section to the car parking area. What a walk of contrasting scenery, from economic forestry to isolated moorland, narrow lanes to small farms. This is Shropshire at its best.

13: Hampton Loade

Gentle walks along the Severn, using a virtually unique ferry service to cross from bank to bank.

Distance: 4 miles (6.5km)

Allow: 2 hours

Map: Pathfinder Sheet SO 68/78 Highley

How To Get There:
By Car: Hampton Loade is signed from the A442 Bridgnorth to Kidderminster road. There is a riverside car parking area.
By Train: By far the best way is to travel by steam train, on the Severn Valley railway. Park at Bridgnorth, Bewdley or Kidderminster stations. Alternatively, book a ticket through from your home station — there are through ticketing arrangements from many local stations in the Midlands. It makes for a really good day out. Ask for Hampton Loade.

Refreshment: There are refreshments on the Severn Valley Railway, and public houses on either side of the river at Hampton Loade.

Nearest Information Centre: Listley St, Bridgnorth.
Telephone: (01746) 763358.

A day at Bridgnorth and a ride on the Severn Valley railway is a must regardless of this walk. Bridgnorth is a bustling market town with plenty to interest the visitor including the Castle Hill funicular, a rarity in this country, the remains of the castle with a keep which makes Pisa look straight and many splendid buildings nearby.

From whichever direction you approach the town you cannot fail to be impressed by its location on a bluff above the Severn, but

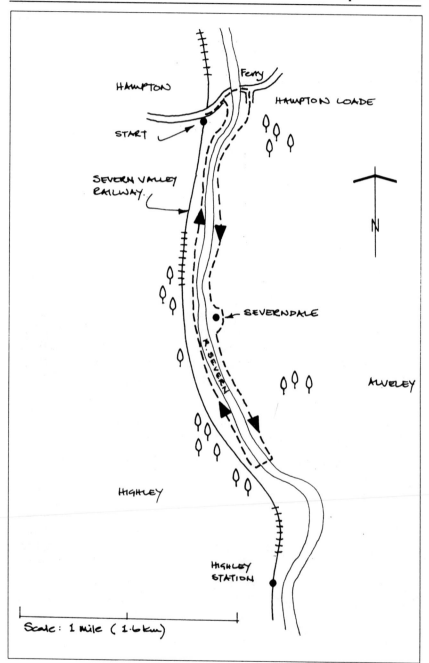

HAMPTON

Ferry

HAMPTON LOADE

START

SEVERN VALLEY
RAILWAY.

SEVERNDALE

R. SEVERN

ALVELEY

HIGHLEY

HIGHLEY
STATION

N

Scale: 1 mile (1.6 km)

drop down into the valley to Bridgnorth station for a touch of nostalgia.

The Severn Valley Railway

The Severn Valley railway is a fully restored steam railway of size and character. It runs daily for a long summer season and at weekends during most of the winter. It was one of the pioneers of putting the oomph back into Christmas Holidays with its now famous Santa Claus specials with sherry, mince pies and of course Santa himself on board! The Severn Valley line is picturesque and in particular, the restored stations are a real credit to supporters and staff. Hop on board for this walk.

Bridgnorth, Severn Valley Railway

Hampton Loade

From Hampton Loade station entrance turn right and follow the
tarmac road to the riverside and ferry. If the ferry-woman is not to
be seen press the button on the pole as requested. This most
unusual survival is powered by the flow of the Severn and operates
daily subject to weather conditions. Using a pulley system and
rudder control, the ferry makes its way smoothly across the river
to Hampton Loade itself, and all for a small sum.

Punitive Measures

Once over go through the car parking area (where you'll start if
you've come by car) and then go right passing by a restaurant on
your left and along a leafy lane to the car park of the Lion public
house.

At the corner of the car park go right and the path joins the banks
of the Severn. The way is very clear. Simply follow the riverside
path through the fields, there being only one diversion away to pass
to the left of Severndale, a route taken by most local ramblers given
the impossibility of following the riverside section here as indicated on the map.

Alveley

Continue ahead for several fields until you come to the concrete
bridge over the river. The bridge once carried the railway to Alveley
colliery, which was closed in the 1960s, but is now a country park.
Once over, go back down to the riverside and head upstream. If,
however, you wish to shorten the walk go left along the banks to
Highley where there is an inn and access to Highley railway station.

Highley

Like Alveley, Highley was once a mining community with the last
pit closing in 1969. It was also a quarrying area and stone was cut
for Worcester cathedral in early times and sent downstream by
boat. In fact, the Severn was used extensively for navigation until
the railways came.

When returning to Hampton Loade, simply follow the very clear path upstream. There are one or two muddy sections through woodland and a few small streams to cross but otherwise the return journey is straightforward. Be careful as you approach Hampton as there has been some erosion by a tributary stream, but continue along the bank once again to the ferry. Retrace your steps to the railway station. Its a pleasure to wait for a train here.

14: Ironbridge

A walk through gentle countryside with one climb up Benthall Edge but otherwise no real gradients. Several points of interest on route.

Distance: 6 miles (10km)

Allow: 3 hours

Map: Pathfinder Sheet 890 SJ 60/70 Iron-Bridge and Telford (South)

How To Get There:
By Car: Ironbridge Gorge is well-signed from the A5 from Shrewsbury and the M54 from Wolverhampton. Travel through the land of a thousand roundabouts to the gorge. Car Parking available on both sides of The Iron Bridge.
By Train: During the season there is a Sunday train service from Wolverhampton to Ironbridge Gorge. Other days in the summer there is a special bus for the Ironbridge Gorge Museums from Telford Central railway station.
By Bus: There is a daily bus, except Sundays, from Wellington and Bridgnorth. There are special buses as mentioned above.

Refreshment: Plentiful supply in Ironbridge and also at Broseley.

Nearest Information Centre: The Wharfage, Ironbridge.
Telephone: (01952) 432166.

Start your walk at the Iron Bridge. As you stand on the world's first Iron Bridge it is hard to believe that this is where it all happened in the eighteenth century, the trigger to the Industrial Revolution. It was not a revolution in the usual sense of the word but a string of technological and economic achievements over the decades which have changed Britain from an agrarian society to an industrial and urban nation.

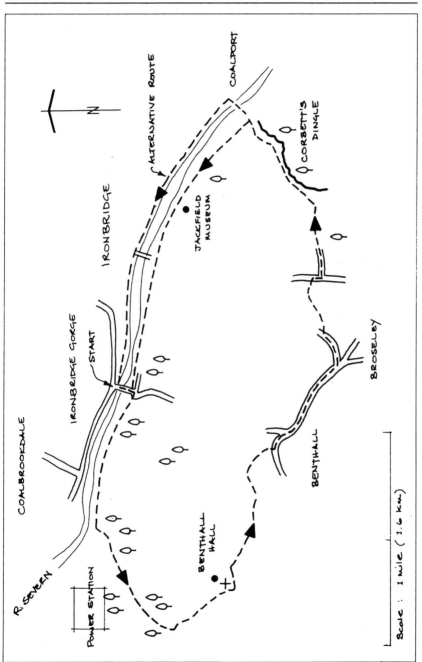

Ironbridge Gorge

The entire area is a living museum of those early days but in particular the Ironbridge Gorge Museums each tell a story of importance. This group of museums and other sites are all in close proximity of the Ironbridge Gorge itself and there's more than one can see in just a day. Stay a few days or return time and time again as there's always something new to see at this UNESCO World Heritage Site.

Benthall Edge Railway Trail

Go right along the old Great Western Railway track bed, now set out as a trail and part of The Severn Valley Walk. The line was built to link Kidderminster and Shrewsbury and survived a hundred years until the era of Beeching cuts.

Continue ahead towards the power station. On your way you'll see the results of the re-introduction of coppicing in this wood. This is the cutting back of shrubs and younger trees every 10 years or more so that shoots become more prolific and the amount of wood larger in the long term.

Ironbridge B

As you approach the fence to the Ironbridge B power station, with a full frontal of the cooling towers, go left and left again as the path begins to rise. At a junction, where a bench stands, go right. You come to another fork and you keep right. Climb up through the Benthall Edge wood. You will see open pasture to the right. You rise up to join a track. Follow this as it climbs up to the bend and curves sharp left. This climbs up to a gate on the right. Go through it and walk straight on to Benthall Hall Farm.

Benthall Hall

You pass by the right of it and continue by the church and Benthall Hall. You come to a stile by a gate as the road bends right. Cross it and walk ahead, with the Hall directly to your left. The Hall, built in the 1530s, is a fine Tudor Manor and family home of the Benthall family. It contains some marvellous furniture from previous centuries. As you walk by, you'll notice the very distinctive stone-mullioned windows and moulded brick chimneys which add character to the house.

Go through the gate and ahead on a tractor track. Before the gate go right along a the line of trees. Cross the stile by the gate and in the next field go ahead with the fence on the right to another stile. Cross this and go left, passing to the left of a small pool to cross a stile by a gate. Keep ahead now with the fence and hedge to the right. Before it becomes a track, however, cross the stile on the right and another soon after to walk alongside a garden wall and fence to a lane.

Jitties

Nearby in Broseley, many of the old pathways, known locally as jitties, have been cleared and signed. It is easy to get lost down them but if you are walking in this area it is worth wandering around these nooks and crannies.

Broseley Centre

Go right and then left Barrett's Hill. Walk up the hill, High Street, into Broseley centre. Continue through the town to turn left opposite the Victorian Town Hall. The famous Iron Master, John Wilkinson, lived and worked in Broseley. He commissioned the first iron boat, The Trial, built in 1787 and developed numerous applications for iron including being buried himself in an iron coffin! The house, The Lawns, where Wilkinson once lived is nearby in Church Street. It is still a private residence with a very large collection of porcelain and pottery which is open to the public on certain afternoons.

As the road curves left, by a large house on the right, go right down a track, which is signed. Go through the gap by a gate and continue ahead to an area of former mining. The path becomes a track again and as it curves to the left go ahead, over a stile, to a main road.

Corbett's Dingle

Go right and then left at the next junction signposted to Coneybury and Woodhouse Farm. At the junction keep ahead and, at the next fork, by the wood. At the wood's edge go through a gate and continue to descend, through another gate into Corbett's Dingle, which is a real surprise. At the junction, follow the path ahead, alongside the stream at first but then moving away to a gateway by a house. You can see the Tar Tunnel across the gorge.

The speediest return route is by way of Jackfield following The

The Ironbridge

Severn Valley Way, stopping possibly at Maws Craft Centre and The Jackfield Tile Museum, to your left back to the Iron Bridge. Otherwise, you can walk under the old trackbed on the road and continue by way of Maws and the Boat Inn to the footbridge across the Severn to Coalport. There's an endearing inscription on the bridge referring to the Great War:

'This bridge is free

O Tread it Reverently

In memory of those

Who died for thee'.

From here, you go left to follow the riverside paths back to Iron-bridge, although they are uneven in places and eroded by the river elsewhere. Either way involves some road walking for the paths are only short loops.

When the writers of promotional literature invite you to step back in time they really do mean it here. The Ironbridge Gorge is a truly fascinating destination.

15: Llanymynech

A borderland walk winding in and out of Wales along Llanymynech hill, with a few steep climbs and the occasional flying golf ball.

Distance: 4 miles (6.5km)

Allow: 2 hours

Map: Pathfinder Sheet 847 SJ 22/32 Oswestry (Croesoswallt)

How To Get There:
By Car: Llanymynech is on the main A483 from Oswestry to Welshpool. From Shrewsbury travel along the A5 then the B4396 and B4398. There is a limited amount of on-street parking off the A483 which is to be avoided.
By Bus: There is a daily service except Sundays from Oswestry with a limited service only from Shrewsbury.

Refreshment: There are a number of public houses in the village. There's a cafe on route at Pant.

Nearest Information Centre: Mile End Services, Oswestry.
Telephone: (01691) 662488

Llanymynech residents must have cursed the Boundary Commission for the village straddles the England-Wales border and so does this walk. The hills here are predominantly used for leisure now but were once the scene of heavy quarrying. This was so even in earlier times for it is estimated that the Romans had copper mines here and, in later centuries, the hills have been worked for limestone. Much of the old mineral workings, railways and canal wharfs have gone or are overgrown. You will see a few on this short circular ramble.

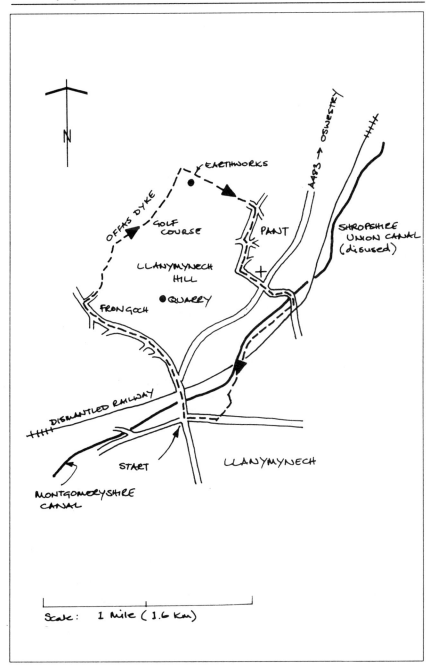

N

EARTHWORKS

OFFAS DYKE

GOLF COURSE

PANT

AA83 → OSWESTRY

SHROPSHIRE UNION CANAL (disused)

LLANYMYNECH HILL

●QUARRY

FRONGOCH

DISMANTLED RAILWAY

START

LLANYMYNECH

MONTGOMERYSHIRE CANAL

Scale: 1 Mile (1.6 Km)

Llanymynech Hill

Start at the main crossroads in the centre of the village. Walk up towards Llanymynech hill, over the canal and disused railway. In fact, if you look over to the right you'll see the transhipment wharfs where much of the limestone was shipped out in the last century. Turn left up a lane signed to Penyfoel, dipping into Wales for a while. Continue to climb along this for over half a mile, ignoring the turn right as signposted along Offa's Dyke Path. The gradient eases and the road curves to the right by a group of houses at Fron-goch where it becomes a track. Go right here up a bridleway, opposite a barred gate at a farm.

Golf Course

Continue up this track to a gate and. Keep going uphill taking the right-hand path up through the woodland. You come out onto a golf course where you go left and then left again into bracken twisting along the edge by the remains of the dyke. As you look over the edge into Wales you can understand why the dyke utilised this hillside.

The path reappears onto the edge of the golf course and keeps to the left-hand fence for a while before being waymarked into the rough again. It then begins to descend, crossing a stile, and through scrub. This obscures the view over Wales. You will probably see, however, a large farm below in the valley. You come to a junction. Go right here through a thickly wooded section, almost like a tunnel of darkness. Do not go left but keep ahead to a stile which brings you onto the course, once again.

Hill Fort

Cross two greens with care so as not to collide with one of those little white missiles. Notice the remaining earthworks of a hill fort to the right. You reach three marker posts. Go downhill to a gate by a house. Go through the gate, turn left and then right along narrow lanes. Turn left at the next junction and then right by a street light along a green track which leads to a path by a bungalow. Keep to the right and then ahead. This leads into an area of scrub and probably an old road into a quarrying area. Opposite the stile on your right go left and the track runs ahead to emerge by a Methodist chapel at the main road.

The Montgomeryshire Canal

Cross over, go right and then first left into Rhiew Revel Lane. Follow the path down to the canal-side and over the bridge just on the right is a stile by a house. This leads to the tow-path of the Montgomeryshire canal, more properly known as The Ellesmere Canal. Go left.

Unfortunately, after a breach in 1936 The London Midland and Scottish Railway ensured that it was abandoned by the 1940s. It is amazing that so much has survived and restoration is taking place along certain sections but very slowly.

Follow this for about a quarter of a mile, passing beneath the old railway which once hauled quarry wagons from the hills.

You need to cross the canal. Just after the earthworks go right and up steps and then turn left. Go through the kissing gate and walk along the old railway. Then fork right to a stile which is to the left of the chimney of the old Hoffman Horizontal Ring Kiln, which can be viewed by going right. This was built in 1899 and ceased production in 1914. You way is to keep ahead to a junction. Go left here and then turn right. This brings you to a small car park by the Waterways depot.

On the main road you turn left for the centre of the village.

16: Ludlow

*This ramble follows Mortimer Trail out of Ludlow to
Mortimer's Forest and climbs up to High Vinnals. It then
descends to Hanway Common where you can either drop
down to Richard's Castle for refreshment and a bus trip
back or, alternatively, walk back from Hanway via Overton.*

Distance: 10 miles (16km)

Allow: 4-5 hours

Map: Pathfinder Sheet Ludlow SO 47/57

How To Get There:
By Train: Ludlow is well-served by daily trains from Shrewsbury and
Hereford.
By Bus: There is a daily bus between Birmingham, Ludlow, and
Hereford. The bus calls at Richards Castle. Daily, but a lesser
service, on Sundays.

Refreshments: There are public houses and cafes at Ludlow, and the
Castle Inn at Richard's Castle.

Nearest Information Centre: Castle Street, Ludlow.
Telephone: (01584) 875053.

Ludlow is enchanting town and you can read about it in the notes
at the beginning of Chapter 7. This walk starts at the magnificent
castle, standing at the head of Castle Square and above the fast
flowing waters of the River Teme. The castle most probably dates
from the 11th century and the main fortifications were added
during the 12th and 13th centuries. The castle was held by the de
Lacy family and then the de Genevilles before becoming a Mortimer fortress. It was held by Royalist supporters in the English
Civil War and suffered much damage at this time. Between then

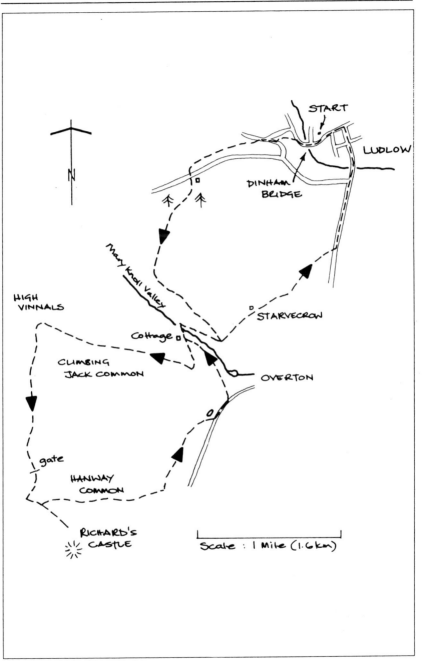

START

LUDLOW

DINHAM BRIDGE

HIGH VINNALS

Mary Knoll Valley

STARVECROW

Cottage

CLIMBING JACK COMMON

OVERTON

gate

HANWAY COMMON

RICHARD'S CASTLE

Scale : 1 Mile (1.6 km)

and the early 19th century it fell into disrepair. Since 1811 it has been in the hands of the Earls of Powys and is open to the public.

Mortimer Forest is where you will find the offices of the Marches Forest District, part fo Forest Enterprise. Most of the forest is open to the public and there are a number of events throughout the year which highlight aspects of forest life in the area. In the quieter parts of the woods you will encounter deer and other wildlife. There is also an interesting Geological Trail here.

Richard's Castle, as its name suggests, was a Norman stronghold. The scant remains of the fortifications stand near to the church at the top end of the village. The views from this vantage point over to the Malvern hills are marvellous.

The walk commences at the entrance to Ludlow Castle. With your back to the castle entrance go left to walk the perimeter walls. The path soon bends left and reaches a fork beneath the wooded slopes of the castle. Go right here down to The Linney. Keep ahead to the road junction then bear right over the Dinham Bridge.

As the road bends right keep ahead up steps. Then go right to walk through Whitcliffe Common. The path runs near to cliffs which are dangerous so be wary. The path bends left and dips to cross a track then exits onto a road. Go right down to the bend.

Cross over and walk along the No Through Road for a few metres but then cut left up the path and almost immediately bear right. This path runs up through woodland to a junction beneath a car park on the Wigmore Road. Cross over here to walk up the main forest track to the offices.

Your way is to keep right rising up once more between tall coniferous trees. The track bends left and rises to a summit. It then follows a main track slightly left across felled woodland. This soon begins descend into Mary Knoll Valley. It bends sharp right and passes an outcrop before reaching the next corner. Keep ahead here along a narrow path which dips down to cross a stream.

High Vinnals

Go left on the track but bear right up the hillside. This reaches a junction at the top. Go right along what appears to have been a sunken lane at one time. This crosses a main forest track and you walk ahead along Climbing Jack Common. The main track bears left but you keep ahead. You reach a fork but keep left to follow the track which bends left up to High Vinnals.

At the summit follow the track as it drops to a junction. Go left then almost immediately right along a green track to a gate which leads onto Hanway Common. Follow the path ahead along the boundary hedge to a road. Cut left here down the Common. If you want to visit Richard's Castle and to catch the bus back simply follow the lane down to the village.

Hanway Common

Those wishing to walk back to Ludlow leave the road at the bottom of the common and go left. Keep company with the hedge on the right for the entire length of the common to a gate in the very bottom far corner. A track runs down to wet ground by a house. Go left at the bottom to a gate. Keep ahead along a very wet section to a junction with a road. Keep ahead to rise up to a point beneath half timbered farmsteads. The track bends right up the hillside and along a hedge. It then drops to an old quarry and you keep slightly right here to join a track and pass by cottages.

The path leaves the track to run through woodland again. It begins to descend alongside pools and down to a stile which leads to the main road. Go left and walk along the verge for a short distance. Go left. The main track goes left but you go right. Follow this for about 200 metres then as the main track bends left go right. This path bends left and soon descends to a main track.

Go left to follow it up to a cottage known as Sunnydingle. Here you rejoin the track used on the outward journey. The track rises up to a sharp bend but you go ahead through a gate and along a bridle way. This runs through to a building and continues ahead to a more prominent lane. It then reaches a stile. Cross this and walk ahead along the edge of a garden and along a drive to exit on the main road. Go left for the last section into Ludlow, unfortunately along a pavement. Cross the bridge into Ludlow and keep ahead through the old walled gate up to Castle Square.

17: The Long Mynd

Hard climbs over this impressive range of hills, justifiably popular, and a place to be wary of in poorer weather. Mainly moorland paths and tracks with some road walking.

Distance: 11 miles (18km)

Allow: 5-6 hours

Map: Pathfinder Sheets SO 49/59 Church Stretton and Sheet 909 SO 29/39 Montgomery

How To Get There:
By Car: Church Stretton is on the A49 road between Shrewsbury and Ludlow.
By Train: There is a daily service between Shrewsbury, Church Stretton, Ludlow and beyond.

Refreshment: There are inns, cafes and shops at Church Stretton and the Horseshoes public house at Bridges. There is a cafe at Carding Mill valley which is open throughout the summer.

Nearest Information Centre: Church St, Church Stretton.
Telephone: (01694) 723133

The Long Mynd is a high plateau disturbed only by narrow ravines known locally as 'batches', cutting their way eastwards. It is carpeted in heather, bracken and bilberry and as such is ideal for grouse. There are also a number of birds seen in Shropshire upland hills such as the kestrel, wheatear and sometimes the raven. It is good walking territory, a place very much to uplift the spirits.

Start at Church Stretton railway station and leave the station from the platform where trains depart in the Shrewsbury direction. Follow the access road to Sandford Avenue and turn left. This leads up to a cross roads where you cross directly to Burway Road.

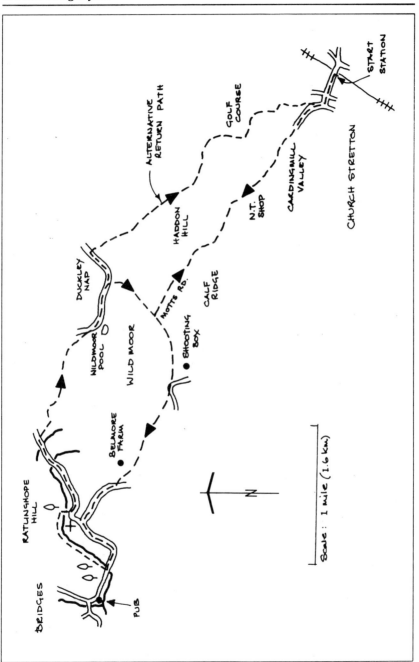

Follow this road, (avoiding Longhills Road) for a short distance as it leads into the edge of Carding Mill Valley. After the cattle grid go right along a track by a group of houses and onto National Trust property.

The Long Mynd, with Caradoc shrouded in mist

Carding Mill Valley

No wonder this area is so popular. The view of the valley is delightful. Follow the track as it descends to the road and continue by the National Trust Shop and seasonal cafe. Continue up the valley, beyond the turning circle for cars and alongside the brook. At the junction of paths do not go left to Light Spout Hollow but continue ahead over the tributary stream to climb up a track known as Mott's Road squeezing between Calf Ridge and Haddon Hill.

Take a rest and look back down the valley to Church Stretton and the hills beyond.

Grouse on The Moorland

Once on the bracken clad moorlands you soon come to a junction where you go left and at the more major crossroads, go left along the green track signed to Wildmoor. This is a wide section of green track and your landmark is short wooden posts to stop four wheeler drivers. As you see this, one main track veers left, three others continue ahead and you go right along a lesser track. You can see over to the Stiperstones and beyond.

This less distinct path crosses others and passes to the left of a pond before heading to a guide post and road ahead, although you cannot really see the latter at first. You join the road as it bends but strike off ahead once again, rising at first, along a path signposted to Ratlinghope. You come to a fine green section as you descend to the left of Belmore Farm. The path becomes a sunken lane and crosses an access track to a house on the right. Once across go through the barred gate ahead. Follow the fence downhill to another gateway and cattlegrid to join the lane once again.

Bridges

Go right and the lane leads to a junction near Ratlinghope. Turn left and at the next main junction right. Descend to a wood and a bridge over the East Onny River. If you fancy a refreshment break then it is not far along this lane to the Horseshoes public house at Bridges just past Bridges Youth Hostel.

If not, go right just beyond the East Onny, across a stile, signed Shropshire Way, and the path leads into the wood. You come to a sleeper bridge and stile on the left by a barred gate. Cross the stile and continue ahead over the track to another stile. There's a ford to your right. You keep ahead, however. Soon the path comes closer to the stream. Continue ahead along the lower edges of the bank into a garden where you cross the footbridge on the right and the track leads up to the road. Go left.

Ratlinghope

The hamlet of Ratlinghope, pronounced locally as 'Ratchup' is to the right with its small church and scattering of houses. The famous story of the Reverend Carr is based on this church. He was travelling to it in 1865 on the night that heavy snow storms decidedly stopped his progress. Having been lost in the hills in appalling conditions for a day and a night he decided to recall the fight for survival in his book 'Night in The Snow'.

The Golden Arrow

Follow this road up the valley for approximately half a mile. The earthworks to the left on Ratlinghope Hill were described by the Shropshire author Mary Webb in her book 'The Golden Arrow'. She spent some time in the area and also described Church Stretton as 'Shepwardine'. Cross two small streams beneath the road and as the lane climbs more steeply go right through a gate up an avenue of trees. The way is signposted. Continue ahead to the fence to cross a stile. Go ahead up the hillside along a green track which curves upwards and climbs steadily to a point above Wildmoor Pool. Drop slightly to the road, pass by the pool and climb to Duckley Nap where the lane curves to the left.

The Portway

You go right here, signed by a lonely fingerpost to Pole Bank, and follow the ancient track known as Portway to the head of Carding Mill Valley where you retrace your steps back down the valley on Mott's Road. Return by way of Carding Mill Valley to Church Stretton. The views are tremendous. The Portway is thought to be pre Roman and probably was well used in Bronze Age times.

18: Market Drayton

Very easy walking along tracks, roads and canal tow-path. Several walks have been written up in the Shropshire Walks leaflet making the town of Market Drayton a good base for an interesting day out.

Distance: 5 miles (8km)

Allow: 2 hours

Map: Pathfinder Sheet 829 SJ 63/73 Market Drayton

How To Get There:
By Car: Market Drayton is on the A53 from Newcastle-under-Lyme to Shrewsbury and the A41 (and A529) from Wolverhampton
By Bus: There is a daily express X64 service between Hanley and Shrewsbury but it is very limited on Sundays.

Refreshment: Market Drayton has several cafes, shops and inns. The Four Alls inn and restaurant is on the route as is the shop at Tyrley Locks.

Nearest Information Centre: Clive Library, 51 Cheshire Street, Market Drayton. Telephone: (01630) 652139.

Market Drayton is a North Shropshire market town now known for the baking of gingerbread. Its narrow streets spill out from the large and interesting church of St Mary and there are a fair number of half timbered houses remaining, particularly in Shropshire Street.

Great Fire

The town was devastated by fire in 1651 and the old fire bells still hang at the top of the traditional Buttercross. Visit Market Drayton on a Wednesday or Saturday when the street market is in full swing and the town comes very much to life.

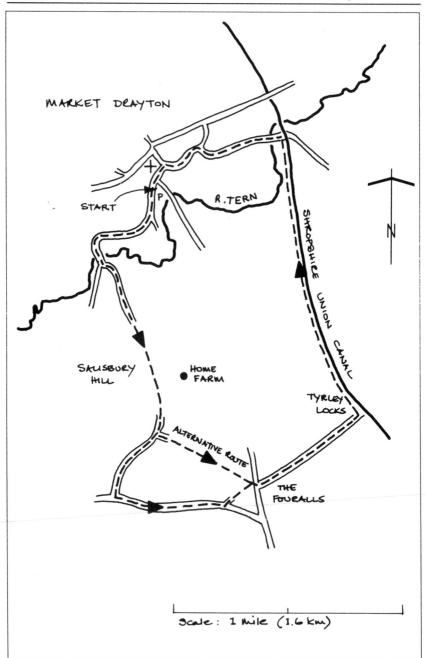

Sandy Lane

Start from The Corbett Arms in the centre of town. From the entrance go left to walk down Great Hales Street. Leave the main road to turn right before a car park near to the baths on a road known as Newtown. Turn left along Walkmill Road. Go left again over Walkmill Bridge, under which flows the River Tern, and left again by an old house into Sandy Lane. Pass by a modern bungalow and the lane climbs through pleasant scenery. Take a look back at Market Drayton, perched on an edge above the river valley.

Salisbury Hill is to your right, chronicled as the grounds where the Yorkists amassed before the bloody battle of Blore Heath, a few miles up the road. Can you imagine the scene?

The lane rises by the entrance to Home Farm and then, beyond a cottage there is a junction. Those seeking a short cut should go left, everyone else should continue ahead to the next junction where you turn left. Follow this lane beyond a group of houses until you reach a track on the left by a small water works of some description which is called Hillside. Go through a gate and then ahead and slightly right to corss a stile. Keep ahead alongside the hedge towards the Four Alls Public House. Exit onto the road by the hostelry.

Tyrley Locks

Cross the main road and walk down the road to Tyrley Locks, which are in Staffordshire, where you will find the Waterside craft shop. Your way to the tow-path is down the steps on the right and then left underneath.

The Shropshire and Union Canal, known affectionately as 'The Shroppie' was built in the 1820s and 30s and was one of the last great narrow boat canals. It was also one of the most rural of the network. In many respects this section of tow-path highlights some of Telford's engineering sophistication with cuttings and embankments being the order of the day rather than following the contours too closely.

Walk along this excellent piece of waterway, at first past moorings then onto a most natural-looking cutting before coming to an elevated stretch as you approach Market Drayton once again. As you come to a large bridge over a road go left down steep steps to the lane and then walk ahead towards the town. At the junction by the school grounds, go left and then left again at the main road back down to the car park.

19: Morville

*A gentle walk along a valley of the Mor Brook. There is also
a possible extension to Meadowley with a very steep climb
as well as about half a mile of road walking.*

Distance: 2 miles (3.5km). Add a further 1½ miles for the extension.

Allow: 2 hours

Map: Pathfinder Sheet SO 69/76 Bridgnorth and Much Wenlock

How To Get There:
    By Car: Morville is situated on the A458 between Bridgnorth and
Much Wenlock. There is some space for parking alongside the main
road.
    By Bus: There is a regular service between Shrewsbury and Bridg-
north with a sparse service between Bridgnorth and Ludlow.

Refreshment: The Acton Arms, Morville.

Nearest Information Centre: Listley St, Bridgnorth.
Telephone: (01746) 763358.

Morville, lying in the Mor Brook valley, is a pleasant village with
a hall dating from Elizabethan times but with extensive alterations
in Georgian times. Morville church stands in the grounds nearby.
It is said that two women and five horses were killed here in 1118
at the consecration ceremony. There was once a priory in the
vicinity but this no longer remains. However, the village retains a
defunct whipping post and a pound.

Acton Arms

Start the walk by the Acton Arms. Cross the road to the steps
dropping away towards the river and alongside a garden. The way
is shown on the map as ahead but the way seems to be by way of

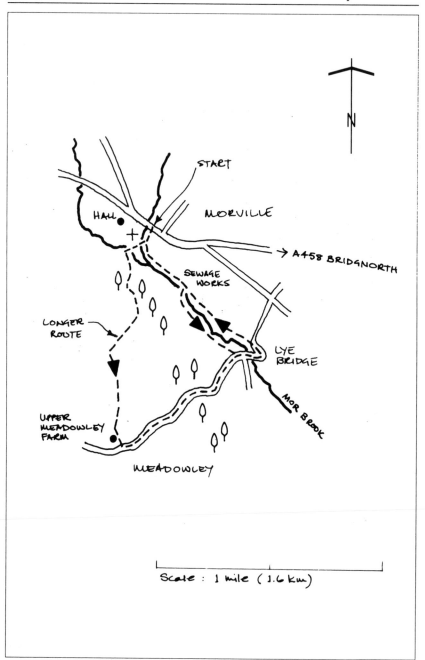

START

MORVILLE

HALL

→ A458 BRIDGNORTH

SEWAGE WORKS

LONGER ROUTE

LYE BRIDGE

MOR BROOK

UPPER MEADOWLEY FARM

MEADOWLEY

N

Scale : 1 mile (1.6 km)

the gate on your right across to the churchyard and then strike left towards the Mor Brook. Cross the stile and footbridge to continue on the riverside path downstream.

Pass by the perimeter fence of the sewerage works and then cross the footbridge to the other side of the brook. Keep close to the bank for the first section then move slightly away to cross two stiles close together. The path continues ahead by the wood and towards a group of restored buildings. Go through the gateway and follow the tarmac drive to the lane. Go left here and cross the brook once again so that you are now on the other bank for the return walk.

Lye Bridge

Once over Lye bridge, go left and up the bank a short way by the brambles and then turn left. Your way is ahead, always keeping fairly close to the banks of the brook, at first slightly elevated but then after the next field boundary, through a waterside pasture.

Pass by the sewerage works, once again, and retrace your steps to the church. From here there are two alternatives. Either return to the Acton Arms as on the outward section or return by way of the hall. From the corner of the churchyard continue ahead to the left-hand building of the hall and then go right along the access road to the main road, passing directly in front of the hall.

Longer Route

The longer route is to Meadowley. As mentioned above, make your way down the steps to the churchyard corner but instead of turning left go ahead to a bridge by a weir. Cross it and go left along the brook's side until the electric telegraph pole where you need to cut across right to a stile leading into the wood on your right. It is not abundantly clear on the ground.

The path in the wood is hard going. It winds its way up the hill to the left at first then curving more steeply to the right. This last section is a hard climb especially after wet weather. A few steps have been put in but there has also been some erosion so be prepared for a bit of a scramble in places and brambles elsewhere.

This wood is used for shooting on occasion so be wary if you hear guns.

Meadowley

At the head of the wood, cross the stile, which has been partly damaged by a fallen tree. Follow the field's edge up to the top left-hand corner. Go through the gateway on the left, then follow the field's edge to the next gateway where you meet the bridleway from Aston Eyre, although you would not realise this for the rights of way in this area do not seem as clear on the ground as elsewhere. Come to two gates and choose the one on the right. Continue ahead along the track towards the farmyard of Upper Meadowley Farm. There's a pool on the right and you proceed through another gate and green lane. Proceed through the farmyard and by dwellings to a road.

Go left and follow this road down to Lye Bridge. Follow the instructions back to Morville as indicated above.

The path to Upton Cressett is also scheduled for clearance and so another circular route will be available and waymarked in the near future which is all to the good as this is a marvellous area for walking.

20: Much Wenlock

A delightful walk through fields into Corvedale returning by way of Wenlock Edge. Approximately 2 miles road walking is involved between Boughton and Presthope.

Distance: 7 miles (11km)

Allow: 3-4 hours

Map: Pathfinder Sheets SO 69/79 Bridgnorth and Much Wenlock and Church Stretton SO 49/59

How To Get There:
By Car: Much Wenlock is on the A458 road from Shrewsbury to Bridgnorth. It is also on the B4376 from Ironbridge. There is off-street car parking in town.
By Bus: There is a two hourly bus service from Shrewsbury and Bridgnorth, and a limited service on Summer Sundays.

Refreshment: Much Wenlock has several places to eat and drink but resist the temptation before the walk.

Nearest Information Centre: The Museum, The Square, Much Wenlock. Telephone: (01952) 727679.

Much Wenlock is as pleasant as it sounds. Its compact centre is full of interesting buildings which in turn house many traditional shops and inns. The Priory was established in 1080 and has had considerable influence over the growth of the settlement. The medieval structure of the town remains today and the local museum reflects the fortunes of Much Wenlock in past centuries in a series of interesting displays.

Olympic Connection
This small town can also lay claim to being one of the influences

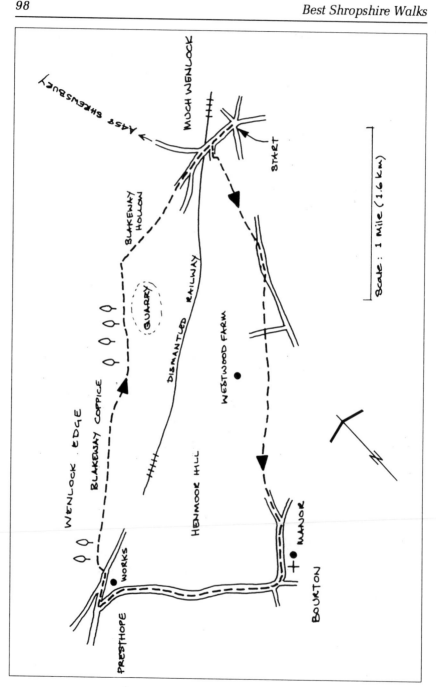

in the regeneration of Olympic Games in the twentieth century. Dr Penny Brookes established the Wenlock Olympian Society in 1850 and in the 1860s competitors came from all over England to participate in the Wenlock Games. Dr Brookes went on to campaign for physical education in schools.

Start the walk at the Gaskell Arms Hotel, once an old coaching inn. Look out for the notices on the walls. Continue ahead along Victoria Road, but do not go left at the first turning to Ludlow. The path is on the right-hand side of the road, elevated at times, and offering a good view of the old pound. Almost opposite the old railway bridge on the other side of the road go left along an alley between houses. You come out by garages where you go right between gardens along a horrible little path to a stile.

Step into the field which is often in crop, and head slightly left to the top left-hand far corner.

Splendid View

What a splendid view of Much Wenlock. Catch your breath and continue ahead, moving closer to the hedge on the left. Go through a gateway and keep ahead again as the path rises along the gentle ridge. Cross the stile and keeping to the hedge on the left curve around to another stile. Cross this and go over the stile on your left. Go slightly right up field and if the stile is overgrown on the left, continue to the gateway at the top left-hand corner of the field.

Corvedale

This leads onto the B4378 road where you walk a short distance to a junction with a lane on the right. Go through the gates here into the large field and head slightly right to a stile mid-way along the hedge in what is very often a sea of corn. Cross it and continue ahead to another stile leading into a lane. Cross this and continue ahead by way of two stiles through a narrow enclosure and into a much larger field with Westwood Farm to your right.

Old Green Lane

Keep ahead to the corner of the remains of an old hedge. Join a track here. The way is ahead which at times is through the retained track and at other points the hedges have been grubbed. The path, however, is still clearly discernible. The views to the left are exceptional.

Bourton

The path soon becomes a lane once again and descends to the B4378. Go right and walk into the hamlet of Bourton with its manor house and Norman church below. As the road bends at the cross-roads go right along the tarmac road to Presthope, a good mile of road walking along this reasonably quiet and very pleasant lane. It becomes a lot grimier as you approach the works at Presthope. At the junction with the B4371 go right and walk along a short distance before crossing the road and turning left into the National Trust car park and access area at Blakeway Coppice.

Blakeway Coppice

In recent years, the paths have become heavily used here and so the National Trust have widened and added a surface to many of the ways. The path curves around to the right and shortly comes to a fork. Take the right-hand route which climbs gently through the wood. You can see quite clearly Hughley church and village to the left. A.E. Houseman has immortalised Hughley in 'The Shrop-shire Lad' even though he got his steeples mixed up!

The track descends and widens. Just beyond this point there is a much narrower path leading off more steeply to the right with steps in places. Take this path up to the edge of the quarry where it levels and then go left. This allows a fascinating insight into the workings of a quarry, not a particularly pretty sight but neverthe-less interesting. There are also one or two stopping points on route with views into Wenlock Dale.

The path eventually leads back into the wood and rejoins the main track. Go right and follow this down Blakeway Hollow into Much Wenlock. It passes old kilns and comes out by the Horse and Jockey public house. Go left here and then right at the main road. Retrace your steps into town.

21: The Munslows

Fine walking over Wenlock Edge between two quiet villages.
Several steady climbs.

Distance: 4 miles (6.5km)

Allow: 2 hours

Map: Pathfinder Sheet 931 SO 48/58 Craven Arms

How To Get There:
By Car: Travel on the B4368 between Craven Arms and Much Wenlock. Park in the lay by just beyond Aston Munslow in the Craven Arms direction.
By Bus: There is a bus between Ludlow and Bridgnorth on Saturdays.

Refreshment: There are inns in both Aston Munslow and Munslow as well as a cafe in the latter.

Nearest Information Centre: Castle St, Ludlow. Telephone: (01584) 875053 or The Museum, The Square, Much Wenlock (01952) 727679.

The challenge presented in The Munslows is very different to that of the 'Munroes' for the south eastern slopes of Wenlock Edge are gentle, but nevertheless offering views of considerable interest. There is a rural museum in the village of Aston Munslow, known as The White House but as opening times are limited, check before travelling. The White House is a combination of architectural styles but dates from the 1350s originally. The surrounding buildings include a dovecote, stables and cider house all from different centuries.

Start from the lay-by and retrace your steps to the Swan Inn. Go left and at the first junction turn right and then right again as the track forks, passing by a small church. Just beyond go left through

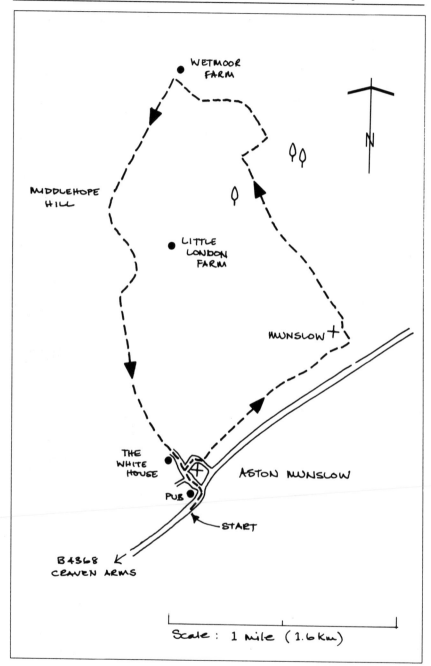

WETMOOR
FARM

MIDDLEHOPE
HILL

LITTLE
LONDON
FARM

MUNSLOW

N

THE
WHITE
HOUSE

PUB

ASTON MUNSLOW

START

B 4368
CRAVEN ARMS

Scale : 1 mile (1.6 km)

a stile and as indicated on the map your way is directly ahead over a succession of stiles. You come to a stile with the hedge on the right and the land use changes from arable farming to pasture. From here the path begins to descend to Munslow. You pass near to a farm on the right and go through two gaps in the boundaries, still continuing ahead now with the hedge to your right.

Munslow Church

Munslow Church

You will get a glimpse of Munslow Church with its distinctive bell tower. The church is said to date mainly from Norman times. At this stage you'll be walking through a graveyard for agricultural machinery and the path becomes less clear on the ground as you make your way down a sharp slope by an old scar. Cross the stile leading into a front garden so please pass with consideration. Walk ahead up to an exit onto a lane, the bungalow being on your left.

Wetmoor Farm

Go left here and follow the road around by the church. As the road veers to the left continue ahead by the cottage and the path leads off uphill. This can get a little wild during the summer months but is a lovely old lane. Cross a stile by a barred gate and continue ahead along a track bedecked by bracken and rosebay willowherb. You come to a clearing and a T-junction. Go right here and soon the track narrows as it curves to the left.

This section can get wet at times, but continue downhill avoiding turns to the left. You come out of the wood by a gate and keep ahead with the fence to your right as you approach Wetmoor farm. The views are timeless in these parts and with cocks crowing, geese hissing and dogs barking it not only looks a traditional setting but sounds like one as well.

Come to the corner of the field and go through the gateway by buildings only to turn left uphill once again, with the hedge now on your left. This old tree lined track leads up towards Middlehope hill, crossing a makeshift stile into the next field and continuing ahead across another stile to go alongside the wood.

You pass over the ridge and then continue along the track, now out of the wood, between fields with fine views of Corvedale, down to a tarmac lane. Go right and then left at the next junction following the lane the last mile down into Aston Munslow. Pass by The White House on your right. It is well worth a visit if open.

22: Myddle

Easy walking, although in some of the large fields the paths are ploughed up on occasion.

Distance: 5 miles (8km)

Allow: 3 hours

Map: Pathfinder Sheet 848 SJ 42/52 Wem and Myddle

How To Get There:
By Car: Myddle is north of Shrewsbury on the A528 road to Ellesmere. There is a limited amount of on-street car parking.
By Bus: There is a daily bus, except Sundays, from Shrewsbury to Myddle.

Refreshment: The Red Lion Inn is a focal point. There is also a village store.

Nearest Information Centre: The Square, Shrewsbury.
Telephone: (01743) 350761.

Beyond the church on private land stands the last remnant of Myddle castle which fell into ruins during the 16th century. The settlement surrounding this fortress has nevertheless remained. It is a linear village sprawling along the road which climbs up the sandstone edge to the main road and there are one or two handsome houses near to the church. The Red Lion public house is a central point for the community and conveniently, the starting point for this walk.

From the Red Lion walk uphill back towards the main road but after the village Post Office cross the road and walk up steps to the right of elevated brick built houses to Myddle Hill. Cross the main road and go over the stile into a very large field. The boundaries have obviously been grubbed in recent years and this expanse can

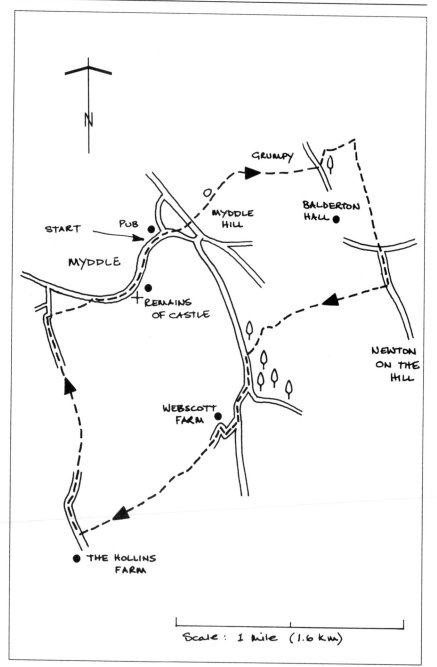

GRUMPY

MYDDLE
HILL

BALDERTON
HALL

START   PUB

MYDDLE

+ REMAINS
  OF CASTLE

NEWTON
ON THE
HILL

WEBSCOTT
FARM

● THE HOLLINS
  FARM

Scale : 1 mile (1.6 km)

often be cropped. head for the middle of three remaining oak trees. Pass by the small pool on your left and head towards the stile. Cross this and go right along the hedge until you reach a stile leading into an eerie wood. You will see some lovely sandstone walling in this area, adding a distinctive dimension.

Grumpy

The path reaches a lane by a house at a place, believe it or not, called Grumpy. Go right and then left along the old lane and bridleway, which is signposted. After a quarter of a mile, be vigilant for a path leading off right through the wood to open fields. Cross into the field and continue ahead over the fields to the road, your exit being marked by a signpost. Cross directly over with care and walk down the back lane towards Newton on the Hill, where Richard Gough, social historian was born. He prepared a fascinating history of Myddle at the turn of the 18th century using the church congregation as a reference. It provides an interesting social comment. Mr Gough, despite being criticised for his work, given its uncomplimentary nature in places, lived to a ripe old age of 88. The air must be good at Newton on the Hill.

Go right over the stile after the second dwelling on the right by the plantation. The path leads to stile and a field where you turn right to continue ahead with hedge a to your right. Come to another stile and go ahead, to what remains of a pool. This is a classic example of an unofficial rubbish tip. Head for the stile which leads to the main road.

Webscott

Go through the gateway and if you wish to return to Myddle go slightly right across the field to a stile, not easily seen, which leads down the wooded ridge to the lane below. Go right towards the village, and before the junction cut through left to the road leading to the Red Lion.

If, however, you wish to follow a longer circular walk then from the gateway cut across to the fencing ahead. Surprisingly, you come to a set of steps leading down into a lovely dell disturbed only by quarrying of red sandstone. The path becomes a track and passes by a house to reach a tarmac lane. Go left and pass by beautiful cottages, which look as if they are out of a Goldilocks story, en route to Webscott. Go right at the junction, signposted to Bomere Heath, passing by a private garage which was once a Primitive Methodist Chapel, erected in 1842. Take the next turning right up to the Webscott farm.

Gentle Scenery

The concrete track proceeds ahead to pass by the barns and turns right towards the farmhouse but then it bears left through a barred gate, before reaching the farmhouse. This lane runs ahead mainly through dairying pastures and a small wood. The track bends left and you now need to look out for an extra thick hedge on the right. Then you'll notice a bridle gate on the right. Go through here and continue ahead to the next gate and ahead once again along the hedge at first but across the field at the end to another gate which leads out onto an old track near to Hollins Farm.

Turn right and follow this splendid old lane, which can get very muddy at times, towards Myddle. After nearly a mile, and as the lane bends right sharply, go over the little footbridge and stile on the right, turn left and head for the houses on the edge of the village. You come to a gateway (look for the signpost) on your left taking you back onto the road which leads into the village to your right.

23: Neen Sollars and Cleobury Mortimer

A very rewarding walk in undulating dairy country. Mainly footpaths with a few road sections. Few harsh gradients.

Distance: 7 miles (11km)

Allow: 4 hours

Map: Pathfinder SO 67/77 Wyre Forest and Cleobury Mortimer

How To Get There:
By Car: Travel on the A4117 between Ludlow and Bewdley. Park in the centre of Cleobury Mortimer.
By Bus: There is a daily bus service between Ludlow and Birmingham.
Refreshment: There are cafes, shops and inns at Cleobury Mortimer and the Railway public house at Neen Sollars en route.

Nearest Information Centre: Castle St, Ludlow. Telephone: (01584) 875053.

The walk starts at Cleobury Mortimer, a small town well known for its church with a crooked spire. The 1828 Business Directory produced by Tibnance and Company of Shrewsbury described it as 'not a place of much trade' but if Sunday morning is anything to go by, when the entire rural population appears to be collecting the Sunday papers, it is quite bustling.

William Langland

Cleobury (pronounced 'Clibbery') was mentioned in the Domesday Book and has always been a thoroughfare across the River Rea. The main street, has a handsome collection of Georgian Town houses and there are also several traditional shop fronts leading out onto

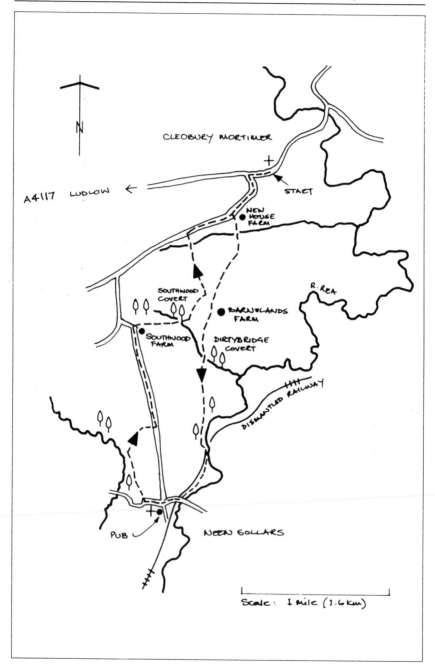

the road. The church is a central feature and has a plaque and a stained glass window to commemorate William Langland, born in 1330, and author of 'The Vision of Piers Plowman'. Cleobury and Ledbury, (in Herefordshire) both claim to have been the birthplace of this contemporary of Chaucer!

In more recent times Cleobury Mortimer has been the home to a local postman poet, Simon Evans and a road has now been named after him. For more snippets of interest pick up a little guide book of Cleobury outlining a trail around the town. It is well worth the read either before or after the ramble.

From the Talbot Inn, turn right along High Street towards Ludlow and at the first cross roads go left into the Tenbury Wells road opposite the Three Horseshoes pub. This curves right by new housing and as you climb away from the village go left by New House Farm, up the concrete ramp to a barred gate which you go through. Head slightly right, keeping to the left of the electric telegraph poles, and soon you will see a track and gateway between pools. This can get a bit messy at times so tread carefully.

Go between the pools and climb up the bank and through the barred gate on the right towards the top. Cross this next large field in a slightly left direction towards the impressive oak, some way to the left of the cottage. Go over a stile here, then the two further stiles ahead. The path is clear enough. Simply proceed to the left of the old building ahead, towards a large oak just the other side of the farm track. Cross the track and a stile, with Barnsland Farm down the track to your left. Descend the field, heading slightly left, where you will find a stile situated to the right of a corrugated barn.

Dirtybridge Covert

Head slightly right to join a hedge on the right and follow this down to a sunken track on the left, as it curves left, in a peaceful valley beneath Dirtybridge Covert. It looks the sort of place that would be rich in game and wildlife. The track bends right and you cross the stile by the gate now climbing upwards towards a small disused building. Go left before this point, again crossing a stile adjacent to a gate. You bear slightly right heading for a point where the fence on the left meets the wood. Cross the stile beneath the hazel and the path plunges fairly dramatically down to the stream but with steps to help the descent. Cross the footbridge and climb up to the stile.

The River Rea

Head down towards the River Rea, a sleepy little river not known much beyond these parts, but which is beautifully fresh and full of wildlife. Continue near to the river banks and through woodland and soon you will see the old railway line. What a splendid line this one must have been. Watch out for the eroded drainage ditch. There's a choice of two stiles here. Keep ahead, however, climbing up the railway embankment and after a short section go left to cross a stile. Then go right and the path becomes more overgrown, winding its way through bracken and descending to the river once again through stinking hellebore and the like. People walk it but it is overgrown in summer.

Neen Sollars

Cross another stile and proceed ahead to a road. This is Neen Sollars, a small hamlet which once had its own station on the Bewdley to Tenbury Wells railway line. It is a sleepy little place with an appealing church but the inn has now gone.

Go right here by the bridge and walk through Neen Sollars, keep ahead at the junction and continue by what was the Railway pub(now Tavern House) and the church. As the road curves left, go right through a gateway adjacent to a restored house. Continue uphill, well to the right of the farm and outbuildings, and head towards the right-hand hedge where you will find a stile to cross. People keep horses here so it might well be fenced accordingly.

Once over the stile, go slightly left to the tree line overlooking the Rea. Cross the stile ahead and follow the track down into the wood and to a fishing pool. Keep to the right bank and go right up to a ladder stile, although most will find themselves at a gate. Exit into the field. Climb up the bank heading slightly left and eventu-

ally levelling out to a barred gate. Go through this and keep ahead
to a gateway leading to a lane.

Southwood Farm

Go left and stroll along this quiet lane for well over half a mile to
reach Southwood Farm. As the road bears left you go right, as
signed, into the field and to the left of the farmyard to the gate.
Head slightly right across the field to skirt the farm and look for
the point where the wood curves right to a small promontory. Head
slightly left down the bank to this point where you will find a stile
which is not at first noticeable.

Cross over this and the stream to climb up, slightly right, and
steeply through Southwood Covert to another stile to be found in
the hedge on the left as the path finally curves up left. It is a bit of
a climb up the stile and field. Once over, head almost directly ahead
up the bank to a gate which can be seen on the horizon. Go through
it and head slightly left up the bank to a gate where the hedge
tapers. Go left through a gateway to the track. This leads you to a
point above the old building spotted earlier. Cross it and join the
track.

Go left along the track for about half a mile, ignoring the junction
to the right near the house. Proceed to the road and then go right
for the return road section into Cleobury Mortimer. Let the crooked
spire guide you.

24: Newcastle

Reasonably hard walking with several steep climbs in this hilly area. A must for those who like to get out into the wilds. The walk includes a section along the Offa's Dyke path.

Distance: 6 miles (9.5km)

Allow: 3 hours

Map: Pathfinder Sheet 930 SO 28/38 Bishop's Castle and Clun

How To Get There:
By Car: Follow the B4368 from Craven Arms through Clun to Newcastle. There is a limited amount of on-street car parking in the village.
By Bus: There is a twice weekly bus service from Ludlow and Craven Arms.

Refreshment: The Crown Inn, Newcastle

Nearest Information Centre: Castle St, Ludlow. Telephone: (01584) 875053.

Newcastle is a fairly large village for these parts with a school, shop, inn and church. In many respects it is a crossroads but most traffic is travelling by way of Clun to and from Newtown. Clun is the nearest settlement of any size with a youth hostel, several inns and shops near to the dramatic ruins of the castle alongside the banks of the River Clun.

This is Offa's Dyke country and many walkers stop overnight in Newcastle on their route between Montgomery and Knighton. The area is dominated by sheep farming and the high hills offer splendid views across Wales. The walk is quite strenuous and takes you through isolated countryside.

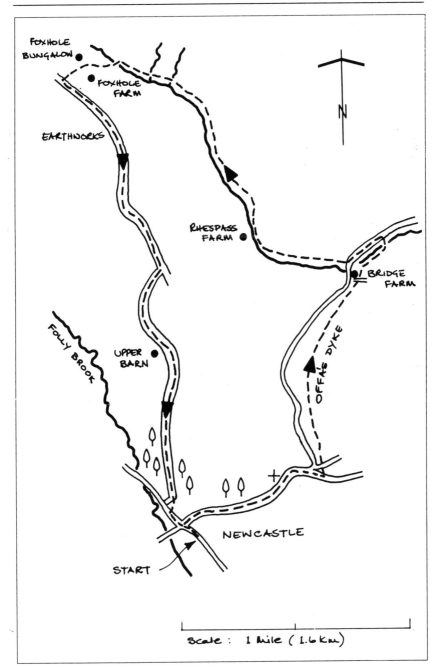

Start the walk from the Crown Inn. Go right to the crossroads and then right through the village and passing by the church some half a mile away. The road bends to the right and you keep right at the road junction. Beyond the cottages turn left up steps and over a stile. This is part of the Offa's Dyke path and is well-waymarked for the next mile. Go over another stile and climb up the first hillside of many on this walk. There's a stile near to the summit.

The path levels and rises again to a brow. Then the path drops dramatically again to a stile by a barred gate. Cross here and as you climb once more there is a good section of earthwork to see. Cross a stile and the path begins to descend once again, through a wetter area and eventually crosses another stile. Follow the path along a section of dyke to another stile beneath an oak tree and then ahead to a stile by a gateway. Go over the track and cross a stile. Bear right to pass by geese and ducks to further stile. Proceed through the pasture to cross a stile and then drop down to a stile and footbridge. Cross a last stile to join the road.

Go left. In a short while you go right along the track to Rhespass Farm but when the lane turns left to the farm go right across the sleeper bridge over the stream and left through a barred gate. Continue ahead near to the stream at first then at the bottom of the bracken banks. Although cleared by the County Council, it is a wild path with not many landmarks. However, proceed ahead continuously up the valley firstly through a scrub woodland and then through another gateway. The path becomes indistinct and wetter as you cross one or two springs and soon you begin to climb more as the valley narrows and curves to the left.

Foxhole

It is at this point that you begin to wonder where you have got yourself to, but the valley opens a little again and there's a barred gate to the left. Look to rise up above the wet ground to a barred gate just beyond a tributary stream. Here a lone waymark indicates that you bear slightly left. Ahead you should be able to catch glimpses of Foxhole Bungalow by a wood on the opposite side of the valley. Your way is to the left of this landmark once you are across the stream below. Look for a barred gate on the left below. Go down to go through it.

Strike slightly right uphill and soon you will see Foxhole Farm. Go to the right of the farmhouse and through a gate at the top of the farm, bearing right on the track. Once through the gateway go left up the bank to join a lonesome lane.

Turn left to walk over the cattle grid and along the ridge with a splendid view of the valley below to your left. On your right are earthworks known as Caer-din Ring. The road curves left then right, passing by a pool on the right.

Shortly afterwards, before the lane bends left again look for a stile next to a gate on the right. Cross this and follow this bridleway, which is clearly waymarked, down by the wood and then past the remains of Upper Barn. The track begins to descend more steeply and into forest. It then meets another track coming in from the left and curves down and to the right towards Newcastle Court Farm. Take the right-hand fork to the road. Turn left for the crossroads.

25: Newport

A very gentle walk along well-used footpaths with features of interest on route. Some road walking on the return section.

Distance: 4½ miles (7km)

Allow: 2 hours

Map: Pathfinder Sheet 870 SJ 61/71 Telford

How To Get There:
By Car: Newport is just off the A41 between Wolverhampton and Whitchurch. It is also served by the A518 between Telford and Stafford and the B5062 from Shrewsbury.
By Bus: There is a regular bus from Shrewsbury and Telford.

Refreshment: There are several inns, cafes and shops in Newport and pubs in Edgmond.

Nearest Information Centre: Picadilly Square, Telford.
Telephone: (01952) 291370.

Newport is one of Shropshire's less well-known towns and perhaps one of its most attractive town centres. There's a very wide and distinctive High Street with numerous Georgian and Victorian houses. The Old Guildhall and Adams House are two good examples. Its most striking feature is St Mary's church on an island in the road with the delightfully secluded St Mary's Street behind.

The town has not been touched much by industrialisation but there are remains of the Newport branch of the Shropshire Union Canal. This was built in the 1830s to link up with the Shrewsbury Canal but abandoned as a commercial enterprise in 1944. Interestingly, the area around Newport was once renowned for its fishing in local meres and ponds, its importance being reflected in the three fishes on the town's insignia.

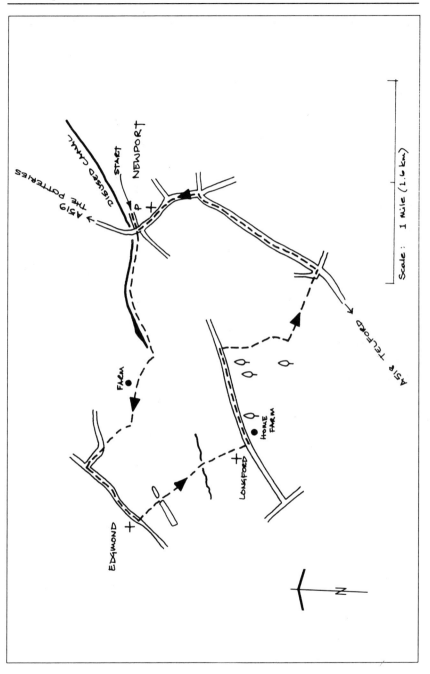

Start the walk from the car park in Water Lane alongside the canal. Head along the tow-path in the direction of the main road and follow it to the last stretch of water, beyond the remains of Tickethouse and Polly's locks. Go over the footbridge here and then walk corralled between wire fences towards the farm. You go left, however, along a wider track until you come to a junction where you turn right towards Edgmond village. Go through the kissing gate by the barred gate and cross over the road to continue ahead.

Edgmond

Pass by the Lion Inn and go left through the village towards the church. There's a lovely water tap with the inscription 'Waste Not Want Not' on the way up to the church. Edgmond is named after a Danish leader, Eckmund, who created a settlement here on higher ground above swampy territory. It grew in size during the Middle Ages but has since remained much smaller than Newport. The church dates mainly from the 14th and 15th centuries. There is an interesting sundial above the main entrance with an inscription: 'As a shadow, so is life'.

Longford Churches

The thoughtful among us will no doubt give this its due philosophical reckoning during the next section of the walk. Opposite the church go left down a road, signed as a footpath, passing by pools to a stile. Cross this and continue ahead curving along the hedge to a footbridge. Keep ahead across the meadow and you'll notice the disused churches of Longford to the right. The Victorian church stands near to the ruins of an earlier Norman structure. Cross the stile and walk up the track to a tarmac road.

Go left, passing by the Home Farm of Longford Hall, and walk back towards Newport. If the lane is quiet you might simply wish to follow this into Newport. If you prefer a slightly longer walk then look for a stile on the right after a farm. Go right over the stile and follow the field boundary almost to the end but cutting off to the left before a house. Cross the stile and walk left up the tree lined avenue. Turn left on the main road and return to the centre of Newport.

26: Oswestry Race Course

*This walk offers a mixture of scenery from gentle pasture
and parkland to thickly wooded slopes. A marvellous walk
with a few steep climbs but offering excellent views.*

Distance: 7 miles (11km)

Allow: 3-4 hours

Map: Pathfinder Sheet SJ 22/33 Oswestry (Croesoswallt). The Racecourse part of the route is on Chirk (Y Waun) SJ23/33.

How To Get There:
By Car: Oswestry is signposted from the A5 by pass of the town.
There are several car parks near to the centre but these are very
congested on market day, Wednesday.
By Bus: There is a regular service from Shrewsbury and Wrexham.

Refreshments: Plentiful supply in Oswestry or the Old Mill Inn at
Llanforda on route.

Nearest Information Centre: Mile End, Oswestry. Telephone: (01691)
662753. This is out of town on the A5.

Oswestry is very much the Border market town, being the host of
Shropshire's largest street market every Wednesday. It is steeped
in history from early times to the industrial era. The Iron Age hill
fort on the outskirts of town is very visible and commanding
although not on high ground. Oswestry was also the site of a
Marcher Lords castle, along with Whittington and Chirk.

Cambrian Railway Headquarters

For railway lovers the station and old workshops area of the town
are a sad reflection of the former Cambrian Railway headquarters.
Hopefully, the Cambrian Railways Society will be able to re-estab-

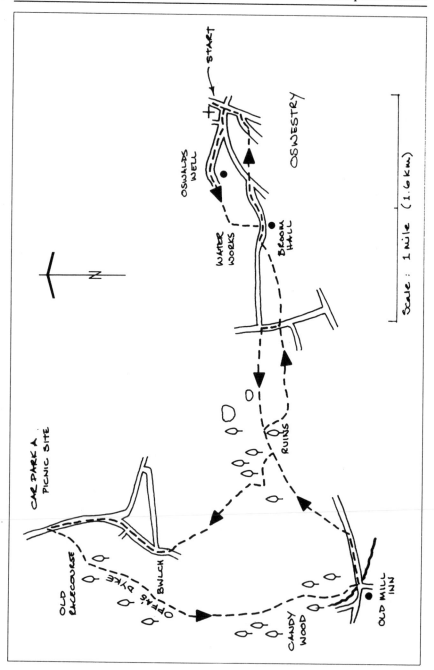

lish a passenger link to Gobowen in years to come. It will be a welcome addition to existing attractions.

Oswald's Well

Start from outside the Wynnstay Arms in Church Street. Go left to the crossroads and then second right into Oswald's Place. As you pass by the school you will see the well and a plaque which tells the tale of the spring. Legend has it that King Oswald, having been slain in battle against King Penda, was carried away by an eagle which dropped his arm at this place, from whence a spring of water has since bubbled. Hard to believe but nevertheless a charming tale.

The road leads up by a modern housing estate to a water treatment plant. Go left and at the next junction turn right. Immediately beyond the cottage go left over a stile. The well-worn path meanders gently across the field ahead to a stile which you cross. Continue ahead through parkland to meet a track and to the tarmac lane.

Go right and opposite the junction go left over the stile. Climb up the bank through an old quarrying area now grassed over to join the fence. Go left and continue along the fence for a short distance and you will see a pool to your right and a wood ahead. Cross the stile into the wood and follow the jungle-like path to meet a wider path where you go right passing by ruins of an old house, Llanforda Hall. This leads ahead to a stile by the walled garden, and another shortly afterwards by a gate. Once over here, go right following the right-hand boundary fence around by the wood and up hill to a stile beneath a large hawthorn bush.

Cross this and go right and at the corner of the field go left, again keeping to the field edge on your right. You come to a stile. Cross this and the track. Go left over the stile across a short length of field to the strip of wood. The path curves left in the wood and then curving to a stile. Cross it and walk up the field's edge until you come to the track. Go right.

Bwlch

This passes by Bwlch on the left. At the road go left, passing a newer farmhouse and then come to a junction and corner. Go ahead over stile by the barn. Then proceed to cross a stile at the top of a field and walk ahead to another. Cross this and join a green track running along a wood above a dwelling. Cross a stile on the left and enter thick coniferous woodland.

The Old Racecourse

This brings you to the very edge of the old racecourse. Some of you might commence the walk from the car park there. Go left on Offa's Dyke Path and continue ahead through beautiful woods on this Welsh borderland escarpment. The path drops a little and curves right to cross a boundary fence then left. It now follows a steady contour for a while before beginning to descend once again, through scrub and curving round an outcrop of rock.

What a fortification Offa's Dyke must have been, using the natural advantage of the land on its 142 mile divide between Wales and Mercia.

The Old Mill

At the T junction of paths, go right then next left, following the signs to a path which now falls more sharply to another junction. Go left and downwards, rather than immediately left. Continue ahead, passing by a cottage and along a lane to a road. It might look like a mirage but across the footbridge is the Old Mill Inn, a fair temptation at this half way point along the walk. There are seats outside and a small garden/play area too.

Parkland

If not calling, go left up the hill and as the wood begins to open up you will see an entrance drive to your left. Walk up to a higher point in he wood and see another drive on the left. Go through it but then turn immediately right along a narrow path, not at first noticeable, but nevertheless walked. Go immediately right again and the path winds a short way to the left to a stile. Cross it and go slightly left upwards to another stile. Go over this and continue ahead in a slightly left direction through exquisite parkland to meet a green track which is just discernible. Head for the derelict buildings and to a stile by a gate.

There are the remains of the walled garden to the left as seen on the outward journey. Only this time, follow the path which enters the wood and follow the path which curves right to a marker. This time go right and come to a stile by a gate. You will see the old gates on the left but keep ahead on a green track down the field. This curves left down to a lane. Cross over and retrace your steps through fields to Broom Hall. Go right down Broomhall Lane and come to the main road. The speediest route is left into town. The alternative is to cross the road and cut across the playing fields to a stile by trees with something of a drop into the lane. Go left and then left again at the main road.

27: Pontesbury

Easy walking along paths and old farm tracks.

Distance: 8 miles (10-11km)

Allow: 4 hours

Map: Pathfinder Sheet SJ 40/50 Dorrington and Cressage

How To Get There:
By Car: Follow the A488 from Shrewsbury to Pontesbury. The road splits in the village and there is a small amount of on-street parking.
By Bus: There is a regular service from Shrewsbury (Barker St) on weekdays and a limited service on Sundays.

Refreshment: Pontesbury has a few public houses and shops. There are also inns on route at Pulverbatch and Habberley.

Nearest Information Centre: The Square, Shrewsbury.
Telephone: (01743) 350761.

St George's church dominates this now mainly dormitory village between Shrewsbury and Bishop's Castle. Dating from Norman times but mainly restored in the nineteenth century, it is a landmark for miles around. So are Pontesford and Earl's hills, the latter having been dedicated as a nature reserve. Pontesbury was once the home of Mary Webb, famous Shropshire novelist who is currently enjoying increased popularity.

Start the walk from the Red Lion public house in Pontesbury, near to the church. With your back to the pub, walk in the Shrewsbury direction. Within a metre or two take the first turn right, and then the first left. This leads to a housing area, library and local school named after Mary Webb. The road begins to curve left, and opposite the school farmyard, there is a rough track leading off right. Follow this until it approaches Hill House Farm

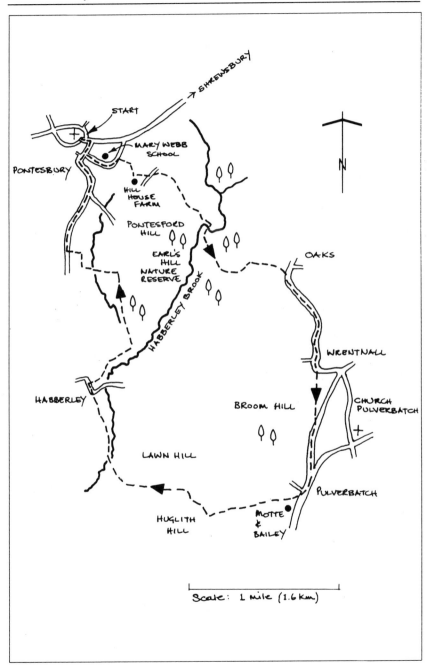

where you'll notice a stile on your left by a thorn bush. Cross it and walk diagonally across the field to a gate. The next section is waymarked. Go through the gate, cross the track and wooden bars before climbing up steps to a stile leading onto a lane.

Restored Barn, Earl's Hill

Pontesford Hill

At the lane turn left and then right onto a track leading into woodland. The temptation as you proceed is to follow a main path to the right which leads up to Pontesford Hill, the site of an early Iron Age hill fort. Do not! Instead, continue ahead and as the path curves to the right go over the stile on your left which is waymarked across the field towards the electricity pole. It then drops to the corner of the field where you will find a stile bringing you into a secluded lane.

Go right, passing by a cottage, and follow the track through two gateways before coming to a third by Earl's Hill Barn, part of the nature reserve.

The path drops down to the left into a beautifully wooded section and meets the Habberley Brook. Just before the small clearing go right to meet the footbridge and cross the brook to rejoin the path at the other side of the ford. This spot is cold and moist at most times of the year strangely reminiscent of the scenes painted in many an earthy Steinbeck novel. The well-worn path, used mainly by local ramblers, climbs up into denser woodland and begins to curve gently left. It joins another flower carpeted woodland track, an area frequented by many butterflies in summer. Go right here and follow this as it curves to the left, again climbing but less relentlessly now. A field appears on your left and as the path curves to the right continue ahead along an older track by the field. This bears right and continues to a group of houses known as The Oaks. The views from this section are delightful.

Church Pulverbatch

You come to a tarmac lane at Oaks, with views of Shrewsbury in the distance. Go right along it to the hamlet of Wrentnall, a sleepy hamlet of character, a touch of real Shropshire. Walk through the hamlet and as the road turns left downhill, go right down a much quieter lane towards Pulverbatch. You can see the church at Church Pulverbatch ahead. At the main road turn right and walk the short distance into the village where you will find two inns and a shop. There is also a weekday bus service to Shrewsbury from here but you'll need to check the times as they are infrequent.

You come by the Woodcock first and then pass by the White Horse, where you continue ahead up a quiet lane with the remnants of the motte and bailey castle to your left. The track becomes rougher as it begins to climb towards Huglith Hill. Part way up you come to a barred gate on the right. Go through it and follow the track up field to another gate leading onto an aggregate lane. What a commanding gap between Huglith and Lawn hills, but your way is immediately right through a wicket gate into the adjacent field and then left downhill along the lower slopes of Lawn. At the first field boundary go through another small gate and continue down the valley edge keeping close to the trees and hedges on your left.

This comes to a point where the bracken-flanked path curves away to the right. Your way, however, is ahead through a gateway but be careful with the barbed wire. Go slightly right towards a large oak in the hedgerow. Cross the hedge by it although be wary of wire again. Then, go right following the hedge on your right downstream until you come to another small stream. Cross this and head for a gateway mid-field, moving slightly left, away from the stream which is now on your right. Once through the gateway continue ahead but keep company with the hedge to your left. Go through the barred gate at the end of the field and cross the track and fencing as you proceed into the field opposite. Turn right here and follow the field boundary on your right to the far right-hand corner where there is a stile leading onto a tarmac lane.

Habberley

This is the hamlet of Habberley. Go left but as soon as you have turned the corner go right over a stile and once in the field follow a direction parallel to the garden hedge on your right until you come to the next boundary where you cross the barred fencing. Go slightly left here across a small field, with secluded houses to your right, to a stile which leads into a main track. Go right and follow this until you come to a cross roads where you go left along a hedged track, gated at intervals. This soon leads into a woodland beneath Earl's Hill.

Keep to the higher level gateway at the next boundary fence and proceed ahead once again through the wood. This joins a main track and there's an access path on the right to Earl's Hill. However, your way is to the left here, crossing a stile and then following the hedge on your left to two stiles guarding a sleeper bridge in a sorry condition. You can see Pontesbury Church and the walk is nearing its completion. Continue ahead in this next field and cross another stile. Bear right here and at the corner of the field bear left, as waymarked down to the tarmac lane. Go right and follow this back to Pontesbury.

28: Shifnal

Gentle walking along well-worn paths with some road sections around Kemberton.

Distance: 6 miles (9.5km)

Allow: 3 hours

Map: Pathfinder Sheet 890 (SJ 60/70) Iron-Bridge and Telford (South)

How To Get There:
By Car: Travel on the A41 and then A464 from Wolverhampton or on the latter from Telford. Travel by way of the A442, B4379 and A4169 from Bridgnorth.
By Train: There is a regular service from Wolverhampton, Shrewsbury and Telford, daily, stopping at Shifnal.

Refreshment: There are a number of inns, shops and take away places in Shifnal. There is also the Masons public house at Kemberton.

Nearest Information Centre: Picadilly Square, Telford.
Telephone: (01952) 291370.

Shifnal grew up as a coaching town on the route through to Wales and Ireland. Inns such as the Jerningham Arms were busy places with coaches calling in at all manner of times. In the last century the first to call would have been 'The Wonder' at 6.30 am from Shrewsbury. A change of horses, a quaff of ale and away it went. The inns are still busy but the coaches have gone. The railways put paid to them in the last century and Shifnal has a central station on the Wolverhampton to Shrewsbury line.

Start the walk at Shifnal railway station, high above the town centre. Walk down the steps to street level and go left, with toilets on the left, along the main A464 towards Wolverhampton. Shortly, cross the road and go right up Park Lane, passing by the hospital

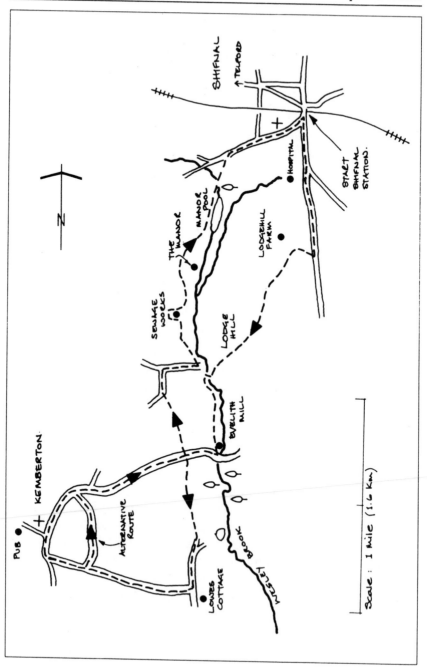

Scale : 1 Mile (1.6 Km.)

and after an equal distance look out for a footpath sign on your right. Go right at this point following the track, with man-made pool to your left, to a gateway with Lodgehill Farm on your right.

Lodge Hill

Once through the gateway go left following the track gently upwards towards the eerie looking Lodge Hill. This leads up to a stile which you cross and then follow the fence on your right. There is a good view of Kemberton church ahead from here, a landmark throughout the walk. The path drops to a wooded section. It is well-defined down to a building made of breeze blocks but be wary not to touch the fences. They all seem to be electric!

Evelith Mill

Go right through the wooden gate and proceed to the footbridge and cross over the Wesley Brook, once a supply of power for a number of mills in this narrow valley. Go left along this well-worn path which rises away from the stream, crosses a stile and leads up steps to the field's edge. Follow this, crossing another stile before reaching an access point to a tarmac lane by Evelith Mill.

Go right and climb up out of the valley. As the road begins to descend again go left over a stile, and watch out for the drop. Also do not take the path leading off in the other direction on the other side of the road. This is the one you'll be using later. It however provides a cut-off point at this stage for those seeking a shorter walk.

If continuing, your path now follows the field's edge beneath a slight bluff, comes to a stile and then continues ahead along a track to a T-junction before Lowes Cottage. Go right here along this very quiet lane up to Kemberton Village. Once in the village look out for turnings! If you're not wishing to visit the pub, or church and pleasant houses in this dormitory village then a short cut can be made by turning first right in the village. This winds gently up to another junction in about one quarter of a mile. Go right.

If you wish to visit the Masons public house, the church or both then continue ahead at the first junction. This meets another lane

coming in from the left and then bends right. For the pub, go left
at the next junction and it is a short walk ahead. After your break
retrace your steps to this junction. If not visiting the pub continue
ahead with the church to your left. There are also a number of fine
buildings in this street.

Kemberton

Kemberton was once an industrial area with nail-making, furnaces
and coal mining nearby. It is hard to believe it now as you walk
through this tranquil part. In fact the colliery closed as late as 1967.

The road bends right after a short while. Avoid the junction right
and the next left, continuing ahead and slightly downwards towards Evelith Mill once again. The path to the left is opposite to
the stile encountered earlier. Go over the stile and follow the hedge
on your left at first. Then cross directly over the field to a corner
and again go ahead to come out at a gateway at the corner of a
tarmac lane.

Wesley Brook

Go right and at the next junction go right again. This leads down
a dip towards Wesley Brook once again and the path is to your left
leading back up towards the sewerage works. Most walkers, however, turn left shortly before and walk up the access road to the
edge of the works where there is a stile to the left. The path follows
the perimeter fence around the plant and over another stile beyond.
You can see The Manor ahead before the path climbs up a sunken
track and over a stile to the left of the old farm buildings. It then
turns right to join an access road which passes by The Manor Pool
and to the main A4169 road back into Shifnal. At the roundabout
continue ahead by the church and this is the most pleasant route
back to the station.

29: Shipton

A lovely walk with gradual climbs through Corvedale and the gentler slopes of Wenlock Edge. Some road walking but mainly paths.

Distance: 6 miles (9.5km)

Allow: 3 hours

Map: Pathfinder Sheet SO 49/59 Church Stretton

How To Get There:
By Car: Travel on the B4378 between Much Wenlock and Craven Arms. Park up in the lay by the Craven Arms side of the hamlet.
By Bus: There is a limited service from Bridgnorth and a Saturday service from Ludlow but no Sunday service.

Refreshment: Plentiful supply in Much Wenlock or en route at the Seven Stars public house.

Nearest Information Centre: The Museum, The Square, Much Wenlock. Telephone: (01952) 727679.

The hall at Shipton, built in the latter part of the 16th century is the main building in this quiet hamlet on the Much Wenlock to Craven Arms road. Alongside is a good looking church dating from Norman times and the rest of the village was moved or removed completely so as not to spoil the view for the then owner.

Start from the lay-by and walk back towards Shipton Hall. Opposite the church on the right is a little by-way which links this road to the B4368. Cross the main road and walk along the lane opposite until you reach a junction where you turn right.

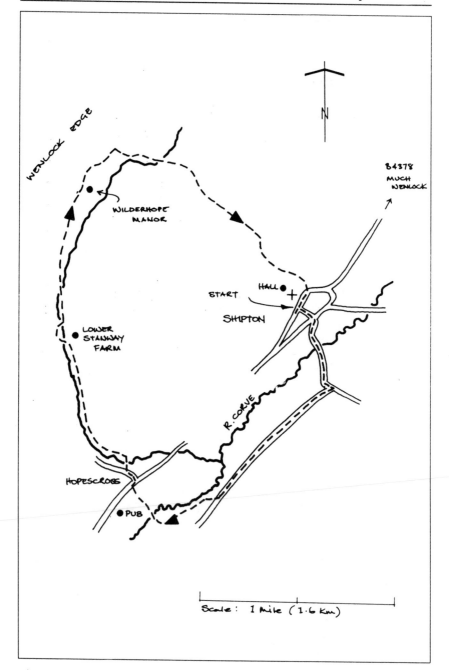

Hopescross

Follow this quiet lane for about a mile with good views back to Brown. You walk for nearly half a mile to pass by the turn to Bowgate Farm on the left. As you approach two cottages on the right, you'll see a Shropshire Way sign on your left. Go through the barred gate opposite on the right. Head slightly left and towards the riverside, passing through another gateway then following a line of trees. When you see a stile cut right to cross the Corve by way of a bridge and continue up the field, slightly right to the top right-hand corner. You come to the main road at Hopescross. If you are in need of refreshment stroll the few hundred yards down (left) the road to the Seven Stars.

If not, go over the road and turn left up the lane signed to Longville. Just around the corner is a stile on the right. Cross it and keep ahead in the field to the footbridge which you go over and turn left well before the dwelling. Walk up the valley following the sweep of the brook until you come to a stile with Lower Stanway Farm ahead. The way has been diverted here and is not as shown on the map.

Go ahead to the next stile but then as you approach the farm buildings go left over the stream and then right across two stiles before crossing the stream once again and turning left over another stile. Continue up the field to cross a sleeper bridge and stile. Walk up to the footbridge, with Wilderhope Manor now coming into view, and once over follow the field edge up to another stile. Cross it and continue ahead towards the Manor. A stile leads into a parking area.

Wilderhope

In some respects Wilderhope hall looks similar to Shipton. This isolated sixteenth century manor is now a youth hostel and has a number of distinctive interior features. It is also thought to be haunted, as more than a few have witnessed characters in the building.

The path passes to the left of the building and leaves the grounds by way of a gate. You will see a pool in the valley to the right. The path leads along the edge of a field to another gate which you go through and cross the stile on the right. Keep to the hedge on the right and cross another stile into the next field by way of a sleeper bridge. Continue uphill to cross another stile and bridge to go slightly right towards a row of hazels interspersed with larger trees. Cross the stile ahead, seated between two trees. This path then dips left to join a green lane running along the edge of the wood to a barred gate. Go left and right on a tractor track.

View of Corvedale

Keep ahead now with good views of Corvedale and the Clee Hills. Continue to walk down the track which meanders by a wood then down to a stile by a gate and then into the farmyard. Drop down to the main road to exit by Shipton Hall. Go right for the lay-by but don't forget to creep past as you wouldn't want to spoil the view.

30: Stiperstones

A walk along tracks and paths with several climbs throughout. Good views.

Distance: 6 miles (9.5km)

Allow: 3 hours

Map: Pathfinder Sheet 909 SO 29/39 Montgomery and Sheet SJ 20/30 Welshpool

How To Get There:
By Car: Travel on the A488 road to Plox Green. Turn left to Stiperstones and The Bog where you turn left for the road to Cranberry Rocks car park. Alternatively, choose the back road to Bishop's Castle, off the A5, through Pulverbatch to Bridges where you turn right.
By Bus: There is a daily service, except Sundays, from Shrewsbury to Stiperstones and even to The Bog on certain days but the service is infrequent.

Refreshment: The Stiperstones Inn and shop at Stiperstones.

Nearest Information Centre: The Square, Shrewsbury.
Telephone: (01743) 350761.

Start from the car park near Cranberry Rocks.

Mysterious they look and mysterious they are for the Stiperstones is an area rich in folklore and superstitions depicted in Mary Webb's novel 'Gone to Earth'. More importantly, the area is a National Nature Reserve as it is of biological and geological interest. As with other Shropshire upland areas it is covered in heather, bracken and gorse with bilberries, and cowberries in places. The views are magnificent.

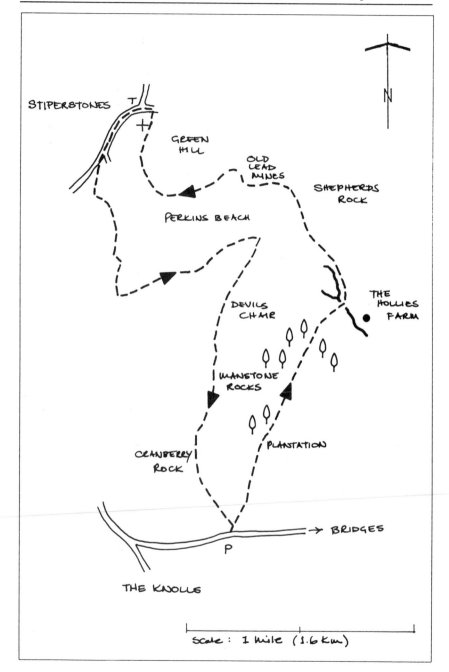

STIPERSTONES

GREEN HILL

OLD LEAD MINES

SHEPHERDS ROCK

PERKINS BEACH

THE HOLLIES FARM

DEVILS CHAIR

MANSTONE ROCKS

CRANBERRY ROCK

PLANTATION

BRIDGES

P

THE KNOLLS

N

Scale : 1 mile (1.6 Km)

Gatten Plantation

From the end of the car park go through the wooden gate and walk up to the Gatten Plantation. The track climbs pleasantly on the border of the woodland and eventually comes out at a gate onto rough pasture with The Hollies farm to your right. Continue to the track ahead but shortly go left uphill and near to the stream as indicated by the blue waymark. Do not cross the stream but continue up to the barred gate. Go through this and continue upwards to a stile leading into the nature reserve once again. The dramatic rock formations look so mystical from this point. Although some might believe that The Devil deposited them on his tour of the British Isles there is a firm explanation for these weathered Quartzite tors.

Stiperstones Inn and Shop

Head slightly right to another crag but to the left of a main outcrop known as Shepherd's Rock. Cross the main track here and take a breather while admiring the views across to Wales.

Perkins Beach

Follow this winding track down to the right at first and to a junction where you turn left down the valley. You pass by the remains of old lead mines. The track continues to curve right by buildings in Perkins Beach, and passing by an old methodist chapel and a little tearoom. It winds down, left, into Stiperstones. Turn left by the telephone kiosk to pass by the post office cum shop cum public house.

Follow this road out of the village and as the road begins to rise go left up a narrow path as signposted. This rises up the bank into the bracken. Go over the stile and turn right for a hard climb uphill by the fence. The path slips to the right of this and then emerges further up the bank to bend left to a stile with a number of scattered rocks on your left. Cross over the stile into the nature reserve and climb again for awhile before the pace eases. Cross over a stile ahead into a field and walk diagonally to a barred gate. Go through it and turn right. Whatever you do keep to the tracks, otherwise it makes for very difficult walking.

Outcrops

At the next junction go left and head back towards Shepherd's Rock but you can fork right well before if you require the short cut up to Devil's Chair. At the summit before Shepherd's Rock, however, go right along the main path passing by Devil's Chair, Manstone Rocks and to the right of Cranberry Rock. This section is a fascinating walk if not a little harsh on the feet. The path leads down to the car park.

Take another look at The Devil's Chair. The legend might, after all, be true.

31: Stottesdon

Easy walking in a part of Shropshire which is popular with walkers and cyclists.

Distance: 5 miles (8km)

Allow: 2½ hours

Map: Pathfinder Sheet SO 68/78 Highley

How To Get There:
By Car: Travel on the B4363 between Bridgnorth and Cleobury Mortimer. Take a turning at Billingsley signed to Chorley and Stottesdon. There is a limited amount of on-street car parking in the village.
By Bus: Not feasible

Refreshment: There are two public houses and a shop in Stottesdon.

Nearest Information Centre: Listley Street, Bridgnorth.
Telephone: (01746) 763358.

Stottesdon is a quiet village between Bridgnorth and Cleobury Mortimer. Its church dates mainly from Norman times and among the many interesting features is an elaborately carved font. The village has managed to retain a shop cum garage as well as two public houses. The Fox and Hounds has its own brewery and after many years in the hands of 'Dasher Downing' it is still with enterprising people. In fact, the number of beers being brewed are on the increase!

Quiet Valley
Start from the Fighting Cocks public house. From the entrance go left and at the junction right. The road is signposted to Chorley and you follow this past the church and a housing estate. The road

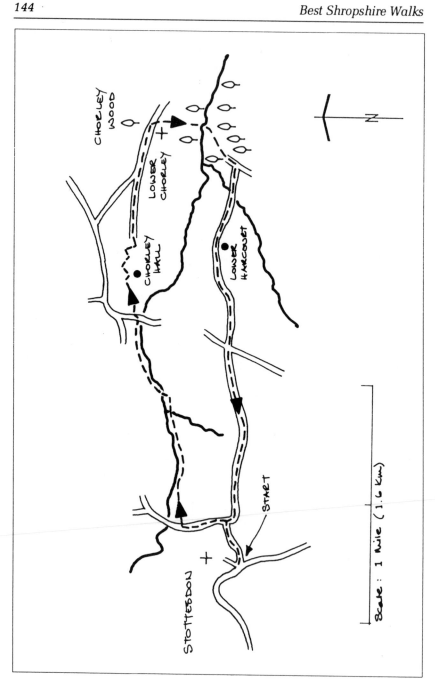

bends left and downhill. Not far down you come to a stile on your right. Go over it and proceed into the valley, slightly left, to a stile at the next boundary. Cross this and continue ahead towards the stream. You come to another stile, and a sleeper bridge. Cross both and continue along this pleasant little path down to another stile, then across a tributary brook with steps up to a further stile. Follow the field's edge to the next boundary until you reach a stile on left. Cross it, go over a brook and at the next stile bear right to come to a double stile. Cross it and keep ahead with the hedge to your right.

Stottesdon Village

You come to a point where two streams meet. Cross a stile and footbridge to walk through the wood to the next stile. Go over this and go right when in the field. Keep ahead with the stream on your right until you join a lane by a bridge.

Chorley Hall

Turn left here and within a few paces go right into parkland. Follow the hedge on the right as you climb uphill towards Chorley Hall. Go through the white kissing gate and go right. As you approach the hall go left along the track bordered by a white fence and then to the left. As you walk towards the gate turn right, along a tree-lined path which shortly bears left and comes down to a track by houses including an enterprising looking post office.

Chorley

At the road junction go right, unless you are in need of a break at the Duck Inn a few paces up the road to your left. Continue along this lane towards Chorley Wood and just beyond the Baptist Chapel go right, not immediately, but along the track sloping away into the wood. Continue ahead, downhill and avoiding turns to the left. The track crosses a bridge and comes to a T junction. Go right here and come out of the wood. At the T junction go right.

The last section is straightforward. Continue to climb as you walk along this farm track. At the junction go ahead and follow this quiet back lane to Stottesdon for about a mile. There are views over the lovely valley as you approach the village.

32: Welshampton

Easy walking along tracks and the Shropshire Union Canal (Llangollen Branch) tow-path.

Distance: 6 miles (9.5Km)

Allow: Two and a half – 3 hours

Map: Pathfinder Sheet 828 SJ 43/53 Ellesmere (East) and Prees

How To Get There:
By Car: Welshampton is on the main A495 road between Whitchurch and Ellesmere. Park in the lay-by on the north side of the village.
By Bus: There is a limited Market Day bus service from Oswestry.

Refreshment: The Sun Inn in Welshampton. The garage sells provisions.

Nearest Information Centre: Ellesmere Visitor Centre, Mereside, Ellesmere. Telephone: (01691) 622981.

Welshampton is huddled around the busy A495 road but despite the traffic is a very pleasant village. The church is of interest and in the churchyard there's an unusual grave of a son of a Basuto chief, Moshueshue, who died in 1824 having studied in these parts. Nearby is the village of Welsh Frankton which offers special country weekend breaks in the hamlet.

The surrounding countryside is rich farming land and there are several walks possible from this base. Start from the lay-by to be found to the north of the village centre. Facing the main road go right along the verge to pass by the old railway station house, then next right down a back lane. At the cross roads go left and after a short distance you rejoin the main road. Cross it and follow the B5063, branching off to the left, for a short distance to a point beyond the old chapel.

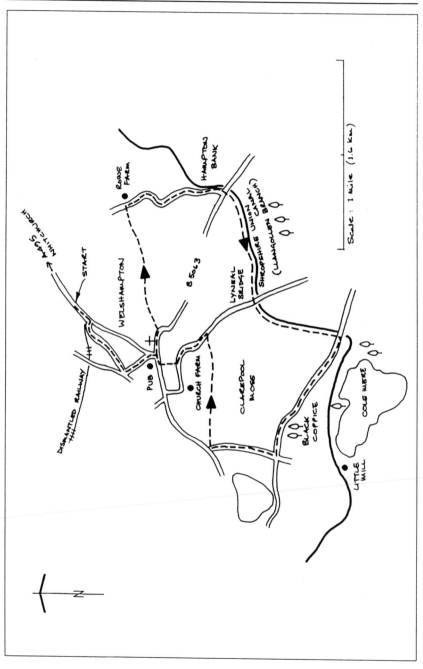

Gentle Landscape

Here you will find a bridleway forking off to the left behind a number of houses. Follow this track, at first open, then passing by a cottage to a hedged way which leads to a barred gate. Go through it and continue ahead with fence to your right and the track leads down to a gate and onto a tarmac lane by Rowe Farm. Go right.

Lyneal Wharf

This quiet lane passes by a number of cottages and soon the embankment of the Llangollen Branch canal can be seen, a spot known as Hampton Bank. The road virtually joins the canal and most people join the tow-path here or a few steps ahead at Hampton Bridge. Either way, go right as you face the tow-path and follow it along a delightful stretch for well over a mile but be careful in places as the path narrows or banks have been damaged. Firstly, pass by Lyneal Bridge, then continue to Lyneal Wharf which is a hive of activity in the summer with narrow boats stopping to check supplies.

Colemere Country Park

Go under the bridge and (at the time of writing) continue to Little Mill, with views across the canal to Cole Mere. Go right onto the lane and right to walk up it to a crossroads.

Keep ahead along a track marked 'Unsuitable For Motors'. This leads back to the main road on the outskirts of Welshampton. The quickest way back is to walk against the traffic along the main road but it is not a very stimulating end to your ramble.

Return To Welshampton

A far nicer route is to go right just before the main road. Cross the stile next to a gate, and follow the path which is signed diagonally across the field. Cross the next stile by a small gate, climb up the bank, slightly right through the gap by the ancient oak to join the hedge to your left. At the next boundary the stile is hidden in a thick holly bush but most ramblers use the nearest gap in the hedge to go through. Follow the path along the top of a small ridge, with Church Farm in a natural bowl to your left. Keep to the left of an oak and water tank, descending to a gateway between thorns.

Once through keep slightly left up the bank in a line parallel to the trees and fence on your left. This leads to a stile in a hedge where there's a large house and garden on your right. walk ahead to exit onto a road by way of a stile. Go left and walk along the lane towards the village. After the lane curves left, you'll see a path, signed, to the right which cuts up to the left of a house to the Sun Inn. Go right and retrace your steps to the lay-by.

Ellesmere

No visit to the area is complete without a visit to Ellesmere, a superb little town bordering one of the better known meres in the county. There is a visitor centre and several places for refreshment nearby.

33: Wentnor

Shropshire Hill walking in a fairly remote part of the county.
Several climbs in open countryside.

Distance: 6 miles (9.5km)

Allow: 3 hours

Map: Pathfinder Sheet 909 SO 29/39 Montgomery

How To Get There:
By Car: Wentnor is signed off the main A489 road between Craven
Arms and Lydham. There is a direct road from Shrewsbury (off the
A5) by way of Pulverbatch and Bridges to The Green where you turn
left for Wentnor. There is a limited amount of car parking in the
village.
By Bus: No suitable service.

Refreshment: The Crown at Wentnor and the Sun at Norbury.

Nearest Information Centre: Old Time, Bishop's Castle.
Telephone: (01588) 63846

Wentnor is nestled on a ridge between The Long Mynd and
Stiperstones. It's more of a hamlet than village and at one end lies
the lovely church dating partly from Norman times but having been
restored extensively during the last century. There is a memorial
here to a family who perished under a landslip at The Long Mynd
and one or two other features of interest.

The Crown Inn

From the front door of the Crown turn left towards the church and
then right downhill but as the road curves right continue ahead
along a less steeply graded old green lane. This brings you onto a
tarmac road where you turn left to pass by Walkmill. Go over the

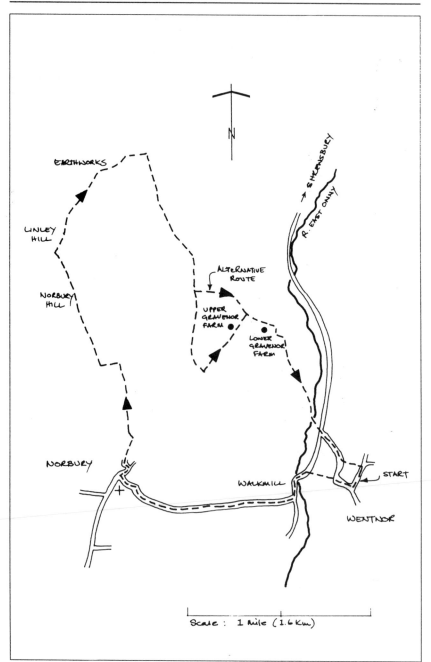

Scale : 1 Mile (1.6 Km)

bridge and in a short distance turn right along a very quiet lane for Norbury.

Norbury

In just less than a mile you come to meet another road. Go right here into the hamlet of Norbury, with its resilient Sun Inn opposite the church. There is a boulder at the end of the sanctuary said to have been a penance seat in earlier times.

Turn right by the telephone kiosk and turn next left. The climb to Linley Hill begins! The road curves right and passes a house. Shortly afterwards the road widens and there is a gateway on the left. Go through here and after a few steps go diagonally right across the field to the top right-hand corner. The views are superb but there's more to come. Cross the stile beneath the hazel and thorn to re-join the lane.

Norbury Hill

Continue to climb and soon the lane becomes a rougher track where you go through a gate and onto a greener section with views over the Stiperstones and beyond. Continue along the shoulder of Norbury Hill until you come to the flanks of Linley Hill, renowned for its avenues of beeches planted by the unemployed after the Napoleonic Wars. Turn right after the gate and go over a stile. You come to a barred gate with a stile to the left. Go through here and continue ahead with the fence cum hedge on the right. Go through the gateway and continue ahead, still keeping the fence to your right. It feels a little more isolated here but the views make this section very worthwhile.

Ancient Earthworks

As you approach the next boundary you can see the remains of an ancient earthworks to your left. Go through the gateway and walk ahead towards the field boundary ahead. However, it is here that you turn right to walk to the corner of the field where you cross into a much wetter patch. You begin to climb following as closely as possible the fence to the left, going through the gateway.

As the path begins to descend, keep a look out for a path leading off left allowing a short cut down towards Lower Gravenor. If you miss it do not worry – simply follow the path ahead and slightly right down to a gateway. It then becomes a more definable track down to a tarmac lane. Go left. As you walk past Upper Gravenor Farm keep a look out for a stile on the right half hidden beneath hazels which you have to cross. (If you have taken the short cut, turn right onto the tarmac lane and look for it on your left).

Go down the bank keeping ahead to meet a track, barred gate and stile above Lower Gravenor Farm. The track curves around right to the farm but most ramblers go down the bank slightly leftwards here and go left at the bottom by the hedge to come to a gateway. Go through and turn right with trees now on your right. You come to a metal gateway under a holly bush and once over continue along the field boundary. You come to a barred gate. Go through to your right and then turn left so that you are now continuing ahead with the hedge to your left. Follow this until you reach more gates and the footbridge over the River East Onny.

Inn on The Green

Walk up behind the public house, The Inn on The Green, to a stile and gateway. Continue to the road where you cross directly to the lane leading up to Wentnor. You can follow this back up to the village or go for a steeper climb if you wish by scrambling up the bank on the left as the road bends right. Once over the stile, walk up the bank with the hedge to your right. Cross another stile and keeping to the right hedge of this small enclosure proceed to the barred gate by the farm buildings. Have you worked up a sufficient thirst?

34: Whitchurch

Easy walking through meadows and along the Llangollen branch of the Shropshire Union Canal.

Distance: 4 miles (6.5km)

Allow: 2 hours

Map: Pathfinder Sheet SJ 44/54 Whitchurch and Malpas

How To Get There:
By Car: Whitchurch is on the meeting place of the A41 from the Midlands, the A49 from the South and North and A525 from The Potteries. There are several car parks in town.
By Train: There is a daily service from Crewe to Shrewsbury. The station is ten minutes walk from the centre of town. From the bottom of the station entrance turn left and follow the A525 to the traffic lights. Cross directly over for the town centre.

Refreshment: There are cafes and inns at Whitchurch and Grindley Brook.

Nearest Information Centre: High Street, Whitchurch (01948) 664577.

The tall tower of the church stands above all else in Whitchurch's High Street. This North Shropshire town has no outstanding buildings as in other Shropshire towns but there are several very pleasant Georgian and Victorian houses throughout the central area.

Cheese Production

Economically, Whitchurch has always been Shropshire's centre of cheese production and several superb farmhouse cheeses are still produced in the surrounding countryside. The Shropshire Blue is a very distinctive cheese made in these parts. Whitchurch is also

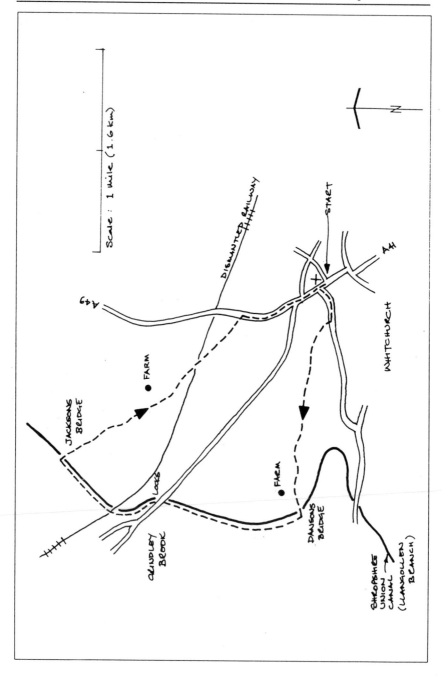

home to a famous turret clock maker and a number of other small scale businesses.

Start the walk from St Alkmund's church. Proceed down Yardington, opposite the church, and then turn right into Sherrymill Road. Before Waterside Close you go right down steps and cross an area of rough ground. This leads to a road at the end of a residential area (by a turning area). Cross over the road and continue ahead adjacent to a garden. This leads through wetter ground to a stile. From here onwards there are a succession of small fields to the canal. There has been development in this area in recent years but a number of small enclosures still remain. It will be interesting to see for how long?

Enclosures

Cross the stile and although there are two paths diverging go for the one bearing slightly right up a gentle bank. This leads through a field to a stile. Cross it and once again head slightly right curving by a garden to another stile in a large hedge. Go over it and head slightly right again to a stile. Then the path leads off slightly left here. Cross a stile and sleeper bridge at the next boundary and aim for the far top right corner of the field passing to the left of the old barn and gaining a bit of height. Go through the hedge on the left (stile broken). Head slightly right up to cross a stile. Then bear slightly left. Cross another stile and you will see a bungalow on your right. The path leads down to the by-pass road. Cross over the road with care. Go slightly right and walk up the drive. Look for a stile on the left before the hedge and go left for Danson's Bridge.

Grindley Brook

Once over, cross the stile and go right over another stile onto the tow-path. Go left and follow this to Grindley Brook where you will find the Lockside Stores and the Horse and Jockey public house. The famous flight of locks here take a hammering every summer Sunday when new hirers begin to make their way towards Llangollen. Walk down the entire flight of locks.

Sandstone Trail

Continue along the tow-path under the old railway bridge and along a straight section, which is part of the Sandstone Trail in Cheshire to the first small overbridge known as Jackson's Bridge. Go up and over the bridge back into Shropshire! Go through the gate and along the fence by the ditch. Cross the stile into the next field and go slightly left alongside the bank to a stile by a holly bush, 50 metres to the right of the white gate.

Go over the stile and walk slightly right over the brow to come to another stile in the hedge before you. Cross it and the sleepers in order to cut across right to another stile in the fence ahead. Once over this go slightly left, passing left of an electric telegraph pole, to a stile and sleeper bridge hidden by a holly bush. Walk ahead to join a hedge which you keep company with until you reach the next stile on the left. Cross it and go slightly left across this field, to cross a stile by a post. Go ahead through the field and walk along the boundary hedge. Go left to cross the stile. Cross it and go onto the railway trackbed as before.

Once over this the map indicates that you should cut across the field slightly left but local walkers follow the fields edge on the left for a short while then cross right along a well-worn section to the track opposite. Go left and this leads to the main A49 road. Go right and walk back into town.

35: Yorton and Wem

Easy walking through a gentle landscape rising to Corbet Wood and Grinshill. This is a linear walk between Wem and Yorton railway stations.

Distance: 5-6 miles (8-9km)

Allow: Two and a half hours

Map: Pathfinder Sheet SJ 42/52 Wem and Myddle

How To Get There:
By Car: Travel North on the A49 road from Shrewsbury turning left after Hadnall for Yorton. Park in the railway station car park.
By Train: Preferably, travel to Wem by train, returning from Yorton. There is a reasonably good service between Crewe and Shrewsbury which stops at Wem and Yorton but the Sunday service is limited.

Refreshment: Wem has a number of public houses, a cafe and at least one fish and chip shop. There are public houses en route at Tilley, Grinshill and Yorton.

Nearest Information Centre: The Square, Shrewsbury. Telephone: (01743) 350761. High Street, Whitchurch. Telephone: (01948) 664577.

Wem lies in the southern quarter of Shropshire's major cheese producing area. Its fortunes were not wholly based on cheese however as it also had millers, tanners and a brewery trade. The latter closed in the recent past and many a drinker curses the owners, Greenall Whitley, for this deed. However, since then Hanby Ales has been brewed in the town and has gone from strength to strength. Wem is also a market town and a number of traditional shops have survived in the High Street. Wem enjoys a Sweet Pea festival to celebrate one time local resident, Henry Eckford, who developed the sweet pea as a scented blossom.

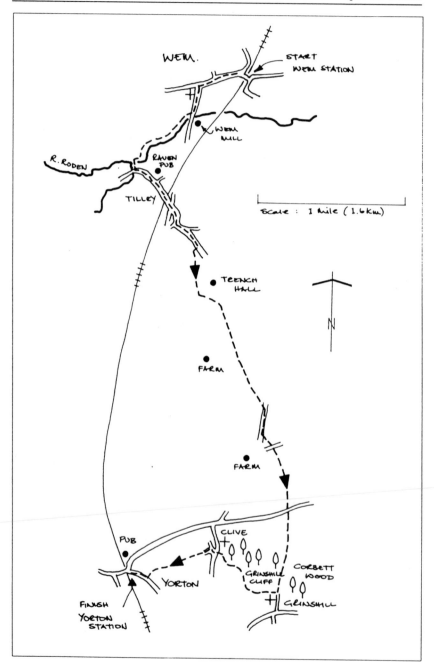

Linear Walk

This is a linear walk, i.e. not a circular. If you are travelling by car the suggestion is to park at Yorton station, catch the train to Wem and walk back to Yorton. It is possible to start the walk at Wem, however, and catch the train back but there is a need for more careful timing. There's always The Railway at Yorton if you've a while before the train is due. This is a must for all those who love a traditional pub. It serves beer brewed by Wood of Wistanstow.

River Roden

From the railway station turn left and walk down the main street to the junction with the B5063, just before the church. Turn left here, cross the road and follow it to Wem Mill, which is currently not in use. Opposite this dusty looking building turn right along a gravelly lane, sign-posted to Tilley Green with the River Roden and houses to your left. This track soon reaches a kissing gate, just beyond a cottage, which leads into a pleasant pasture. Follow the river's edge until you come to a bridge. Go over it and keep right to walk the short distance along a fenced path up to the gate leading at the road.

The Village of Tilley

Turn left here and pass through the village of Tilley with the Raven pub on your left and an imposing black and white building virtually opposite dating from 1613. As the road bends to the left continue ahead along a 'No Through Road' which leads to the railway line. Cross the tracks with extreme caution and then walk the second half of the truncated lane to the main B5476 road. Cross the road to the lane opposite, signed to Tilley Green.

Shropshire Way

Pass by a group of houses and as the road bears left continue ahead along another 'No Through Road'. Immediately beyond the house on the left there is a stile on the right. Cross it and go through a narrow enclosure heading slightly left to the next stile. Cross this and head in the direction indicated by the stile across a very large field, with Trench Hall appearing more clearly to your left. Mid-field you'll see the wooden fencing in the thick boundary hedge. Cross this and then walk slightly left again across a field which has markers to guide you to the next field. Cross the stile and your way becomes far clearer following at first the hedge to the left until you come to a gateway under a sycamore tree. Cross this and a succession of fields, keeping to the hedge on your right, until you eventually come to a green lane. This is very much dairying country and so be on the look out for the occasional bull. The electric fencing can also be a minor irritation.

Corbet Woods

Turn right into the lane and in a short distance look for a waymark to your left by an iron gate. Go through the gate and follow the hedge on the right to the stile by the pool. Cross it and continue along the fields edge to meet a track. Cross this and go over the stile. Your way is ahead, passing by a pool on your left, move gradually to a stile in the far top left-hand corner of the field. Cross it and a sleeper bridge across the ditch into the next field where you continue ahead to the tarmac lane. Cross the road and cross the stile, and head up the field with the hedge on your right. Cross the stile and go left up the hill to a stile leading by a cottage and into the woods.

Quarrying

Once at the track, cross over and go slightly left to find a little path dipping down through the woodland. Go left at the first fork and as soon as you meet a main path go right downhill more steeply through a cutting. The area was once famous for its quarries with stone being used in Shrewsbury and further afield. Much of this is overgrown now and rich in wildlife.

This leads down to the village hall where you turn left for a look at the church, and if you are calling at the Elephant and Castle pub, left again at the junction. It is only a matter of a minutes walk.

If not, turn right by the Jubilee Oak planted in 1935 by Miss Cynthia Bibby, sheltering a seat for the weary on their travels! This is a lovely old sandstone track linking a number of houses lying beneath Grinshill Cliff with splendid views across the fields.

Clive

It comes out at Clive church, a considerable landmark for miles around, near to Clive Hall dating from Elizabethan times. Turn left at the church and then first right, passing by a village hall. Continue ahead if you need to call into the village stores, otherwise your way is first left along an old track which can get a little overgrown in summer so a stick is handy here at times. This emerges into a field where you continue downhill with the hedge being on your right. Go through the gate and cross the stile ahead.

The path is ahead once again to the 5 barred gate which leads onto the tarmac lane. Go right to Yorton Railway Station. To your left across the fields is Sansan House and gardens. The latter are open on occasions to raise funds for charity. Check with tourist information before travelling. The access to Yorton station is on your left but peep around the corner at the Railway Inn first – it is a delightful old pub! The entrance is at the side (open at lunchtimes and from 7 pm in the evenings).

36: The Wrekin

Shropshire's favourite hill with steep climbs and descents.
Superb views.

Distance: 6 miles (9.5Km)

Allow: 3 hours

Map: Pathfinder Sheet 890 SJ 60/70 Iron-Bridge and Telford (South)

How To Get There:
> By Car: From Shrewsbury (A5) or Birmingham (M54) follow signs to
> Wellington (B5061) and then The Wrekin. Park at Forest Glen.
> By Train: There is a daily service from Shrewsbury and Wolverhamp-
> ton to Wellington (Telford West). It is a good hour's walk through the
> town and along back lanes to Forest Glen. The bus is infrequent.

Refreshment: Several shops, inns and cafes in Wellington or Ironbridge.

Nearest Information Centre: The Wharfage, Ironbridge.
Telephone: (01952) 432166.

The Wrekin must surely be Shropshire's most famous hill and as
with many of the others is surrounded in folklore and mystery. In
fact, a giant might have had something to do with its existence in
the first place if you believe one such yarn. It is in fact, one of the
oldest Pre-Cambrian ranges in Britain and is volcanic in origin. It
is only 1334 feet high but being surrounded by lowlands seems
much higher. The views, nevertheless, are magnificent.

From the Forest Glen road junction walk up past the toilet block
into the wood along a wide track which winds around to the right
and then after a while look for the turning off to the right. Pass by
Wrekin Cottage and then the track veers left uphill towards the

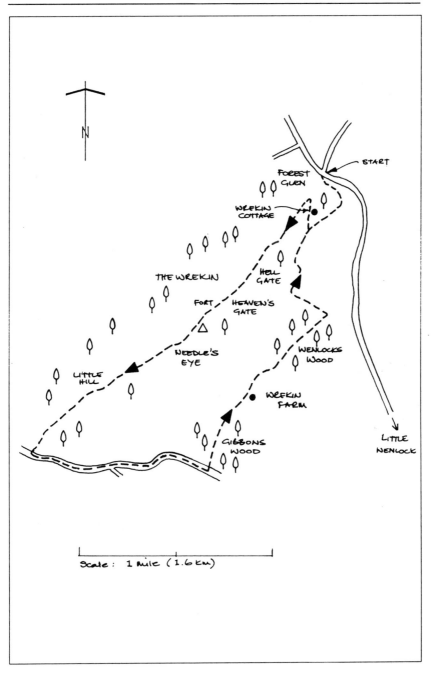

summit. There are several notices warning of the danger of walks on the western slopes when firing practice is in motion.

From Hell to Heaven

The path rises to the northern section of the ramparts of an ancient fort. This is known as Hell Gate, so pass through gingerly. The next section is Heavens's Gate so stroll serenely here and then pass the summit at the trig point before descending through the Needle's Eye to a wooded path which is steep in places. The latter place is thought to have been the home of a medieval hermit.

You come to a natural gap where you continue ahead climbing a much gentler slope to the appropriately named Little Hill. At the top there are several paths to choose from. Keep ahead, clambering down a path slightly left into the woodland below. Avoid all cross paths but maintain a path ahead through thick woodland to a stile which exits onto a tarmac lane.

Gibbons Wood

Go left and follow this lane for about a mile, passing by a few farms. Pass by the entrance to the scout camp and then alongside two farms, go left opposite a house, through a gap stile by a barred gate. Walk up through Gibbons Wood and go over the stile leading into a field offering fine views of The Wrekin. Keep ahead, with the hedge to your right and cross another stile. Proceed ahead along the track as you pass Wrekin Farm.

Follow this track which soon leads into Wenlocks Wood and at the far end go left over the stile, walking up the field's edge. Cross another stile and climb up the small enclosure to the main path where you go right. This woodland path joins the junction where you first began to climb up The Wrekin. This time, continue ahead to retrace your steps to Forest Glen.

SNOWDONIA ROCKY RAMBLES
Geology Beneath your Feet

Bryan Lynas

This is a guidebook with a huge difference: learn about the rocks and scenery of Snowdonia as you enjoy some excellent rambles. Background text describes why the area looks as it does. Learn about the tremendous forces that shaped the earth, imagine huge volcanoes, picture the deep seas!

(£9.95)

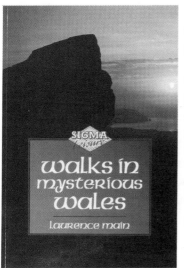

WALKS IN MYSTERIOUS WALES

Laurence Main

Follow the spirit paths of Wales - visit the most sacred and secret sites and discover ancient traditions of this historic country in the company of a leading expert. And, while you're discovering Welsh heritage, enjoy some excellent walks across the length and breadth of the country.

(£7.95)

HILL WALKS IN MID WALES
The Cambrian Mountains

Dave Ing

This is one of the very few books to explore the pleasures of walking in Mid Wales - far from from the big mountains of Snowdonia and away from the crowds, yet so accessible for a day in the hills.

(£7.95)

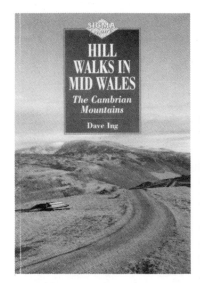